THE FORGET-ABOUT-IT GUIDE™
TO BETTER GOLF

HOW TO LOWER YOUR SCORES BY LIMITING WHAT YOU LEARN.
BY JOHN FURGURSON & ANDY HEINLY

Cover Concept by Tom Kelly & John Furgurson
Book Design by Dave Caplan
Cover Design by Carlos Perez
Cover photo by Mike Houska, Dogleg Studios
Printed in the United States

Forget-About-It Books are published by 2E Publishing
1293 NW Wall St. #1336 Bend, Oregon 97701

ISBN 0-9752602-0-0
LCCN 2004094941
forgetaboutitgolf.com

*To our kids, who continually demonstrate
the joy and power of pure, unadulterated play. And to
Laura and Nancy for their infinite love, patience, and support.*

TABLE OF CONTENTS

FOREWORD
By Wally Armstrong

Golf has been a part of my life for as long as I can remember. Once you catch the bug it never leaves you. I've had the privilege of playing on the PGA tour in over 300 events around the world and I only wish I had read this book before hitting the tour in 1974. Every golfer from the beginner to the tour player needs to have a grasp of the truths that John and Andy lay out in this fabulous book.

They really hit the nail on the head when they describe how the average golfer gets totally wrapped up in the mechanics of the game, to the point where he can't even hit the ball. There's an old saying that I often quote to my students. It goes like this: "*A centipede was happy quite, until a toad in fun said, 'Pray which leg goes after which?' This put his mind in such a pitch, he lay distracted in a ditch, considering how to run.*"

Walter Hagan once said "you have to be a little dumb to be a good golfer." That is, you have to learn to turn off the thinking. As John and Andy put it, you have to forget about the "brain" and rely on the trusting "player" inside you. It's a masterful way of describing those two friendly adversaries.

When I teach, my goal is to find the golfer inside of every student and draw him out. That is what this book is all about. By telling you to "forget about it" John and Andy are imploring readers to enjoy playing the game without getting caught up coordinating a swing. Their book equips you to enjoy the learning process and to understand how to apply the learning to playing the game with freedom and confidence. In essence: be engaged in shot playing rather then swing development.

J. H. Taylor winner of a number of British Opens at the turn-of-the-century wrote "there cannot be a fluid natural swing when the mind is involved in instructing the body." That pretty much sums it up.

This book covers all the bases, or should I say the holes. It gives you a wonderful understanding of how to learn the game and how to find a good, compatible instructor. (That's one investment that can't lose.) They also have insights into how to make practice fun and enjoyable. Just as John learned the feel of the correct golf swing by simply swinging a plastic ball on a string. That's the essence of Forget-About-It golf.

You see, you develop feelings in practice and then when you're out on the course you just trust those feelings and let them flow. Training tools allow you to gain the feelings of the correct positions without becoming mechanically engaged. And that, my friend, produces the freedom to freewheel the ball down the fairway, onto the green then into the hole. Sounds easy doesn't it? Well it can be for anyone who reads and digests the words on the pages following this humble forward.

You are going to love reading this book because it gives you so many solid ways of approaching the total game. John and Andy reveal time tested insights that will help you increase your enjoyment of the game forever. Three simple truths are covered: I. Quit trying so hard and have fun out there. 2. Minimize your mistakes by winning the head game 3. Sharpen your short game.

Not only do they cover all of these truths, but there's more. I love their section on building a routine and how this enhances your tempo and rhythm. Andy likes to call it the three R's… routine plus rhythm equals reward. And if you have no rhythm, you have no game.

The book concludes with some tasty tidbits of putting expertise. You'll step right inside John's mind and see how he overcame the dreaded disease that they called in the old days "YARDPUT-TAPHOBIA". Wouldn't you like to look at the hole as if it were a manhole on Madison Avenue? Well, you can, and that is what makes golf fun. And that's what this book is all about. Just forget about it and enjoy the "game of games".

One last thing. If you're ever within three states of Central Oregon, you have got to call Andy for a lesson or two!

AUTHOR'S NOTE

I have to start with a disclaimer: I'm a better writer than I am a golfer. I have no credentials as a PGA pro. I'm not a perennial pro-am participant or a club champion. In fact, for most of my life I hacked it around with all of you who struggle to break 90.

But about five years ago, when I had way too much time on my hands, I managed to sharpen up my game considerably. With a couple of well-timed lessons, a lot of reading, and tons of practice, I whittled my USGA handicap index to a respectable 6.9.

Inevitably, it didn't last long. In hindsight, I know I was trying way too hard to live up to the expectations that come with a single-digit handicap. And the harder I tried, the worse I got.

I was what you would call an over-informed underachiever. In an effort to maintain my handicap, I studied the works of Nicklaus, Hogan and Jones. I read Dave Pelz's books. I tried David Lee's Gravity Golf method. I researched Mo Norman and the Natural Golf method. You name it, I tried it. I was experimenting constantly, and I was learning a lot, but I just wasn't getting any better. In fact, I was going backwards. Basically, I knew way too much for my own good.

Pretty soon my game was in a shambles; I caught a debilitating case of the yips, my dependable old swing was lost in a fog of confusion and worst of all, I wasn't enjoying myself. I was trying so hard, every round felt like an epic ascent up Mt. Everest. And I was out of oxygen.

Then I saw Andy Heinly do one of his clinics. He was entertaining. He was humble. And he demonstrated rather dramatically that I was making the game way more complicated than it needed to be.

I went into our first lesson together with all sorts of theories about what I was doing wrong and what I needed to work on. But as I tried to explain my ideas to Andy he just looked me in the eye, nodded, and said "Forget about it. If you want me to help, you have to forget about all that junk you've been reading and just trust me."

Needless to say, I was skeptical. I'd spent years studying the game and I was quite sure I knew my own swing. But I played along, and by the end of the hour I was sold — hook, line and sinker.

Andy didn't spend the time explaining all my problems. (I had more bad habits than a flea-ridden mutt.) Instead, he helped me forget about them. He helped me shift my thinking entirely and immediately got me going in the right direction... straight toward the target.

Andy boiled it all down into something I could get my head around. He simplified the process dramatically and directed me gently toward my natural swing. He seemed to have an instinctive ability to zero-in on solutions to the underlying problem, not just the symptoms. And he did it all without talking my ear off or filling my head with a half dozen new swing thoughts.

Suddenly I was hitting my irons dead center in the middle of the clubhead. For the first time in my life I could relate to the old adage; "effortless force, not forceful effort." Everything seemed easier. My pitches were settling closer to the hole. And even the putts started to find the target. Without consciously trying, without thinking about my swing one bit, I was improving everything I did on the golf course.

That was not the first good golf lesson I ever had, but it was the first one where I felt like I wasn't going to get a lot worse before I got better. Under Andy's tutelage I knew I could go straight out to the course and apply what I learned, without worrying about all sorts of little swing details. For the first time in years, my mind was uncluttered enough to learn effectively.

The overwhelming sense of freedom and relief I experienced from that first lesson was my inspiration for this book. After years of frustration, Andy proved to me that golf doesn't have to be a grind and that you can, in fact, learn to play well without getting into physics, geometry or biomechanics. And somebody needs to spread the word.

Thousands of people quit this game every year, simply out of frustration. The learning curve is just too overwhelming for a lot of people. But it doesn't have to be.

The Forget-About-It Guide To Better Golf was written and conceived specifically to ease the frustration that so many of us experience in this game. It's a welcome departure from the usual "how-to-swing-a-club-my-way" books and is based on one fundamental truth: What you don't work on (i.e. worry about) is often more important than what you do work on.

The focus is not on improving your golf swing, per se, but on improving your game. It's a mindset more than a method. It's a process of illumination, not elimination. To borrow Dr. Bob Roetella's words, it's about getting out of the training mindset and into the trusting mindset.

The Forget-About-It Guide will show you how conflicting technical information prevents you from performing up to your potential. For instance, you've probably been told to keep your left arm straight and your eye on the ball. Well, forget about it. You know that rule that says the perfect putt should finish 16 inches past the cup? You can forget about that one too. Cupping your left wrist, uncoiling the left hip, un-weighting the baby toe of the left foot. Forget about it, forget about it, forget about it!

If you're looking for swing tips and technical information, look somewhere else. This is not The Five Fundamentals by Ben Hogan. On the contrary. There's no talk of spine angles and swing planes. There's no debate about the overlap grip versus the interlocking grip. And most of all, there are no immutable laws for you to follow.

Andy and I don't have all the answers. But we do have some practical advice that will help you recognize the tips that do — and more importantly, do not — apply to your game. This is one of the few golf books that can actually cure "paralysis by analysis," rather than contribute to it. So put aside all the other advice and stay focused on what's important: the target, the object of the game, and having fun.

I'm not sure what has helped me more, Andy's instruction or the process of writing this book. But this much I know: I'm having more fun on the golf course than I've ever had. I'm more confident than I have been in years, and even when I'm not scoring particularly well, I'm enjoying the ride. Because for the first time, I know the scores will come. If I can only forget about it and play.

INTRODUCTION
By Andy Heinly

In 1996, when I was at Pumpkin Ridge near Portland, Tiger Woods came to town for the U.S. Amateur. Even then he commanded massive media attention, and when he came from behind to win his third consecutive title, I knew things were going to change. You could feel the wave rising in our sport. New courses were popping up everywhere, TV ratings were going way up, and a lot of people were taking up the game. Up, up up. It was an exciting time to be in the business, but you know what? It was bound to come back down at some point.

The wave has crested and we're once again looking at a sport that's not really growing. Many people who took up the game in that post-Tiger boom have given up. Either they discovered they didn't have the time, or they were too intimidated, or they played for awhile and got so frustrated they just said "heck with it." I've seen it all.

As a Head Pro or Director Of Golf you have to wear a lot of different hats. Tournament Director, Pro Shop Manager, Counsellor, Boss. But my favorite role, by far, has always been Instructor. I love being a coach, teacher and mentor, and in that role, I believe my foremost responsibility is to help people get more enjoyment out of the game.

If they're beginners, my goal is simply to put them at ease. I introduce them to the culture of golf and give just enough instruction to pique their interest, without scaring them off. The last thing

I want to do is boggle their minds with all sorts of technical advice that they won't understand, much less apply.

Then there are the frustrated under-achievers, like my co-author. Guys like John get so wrapped up in how to swing, I have to surgically remove the instruction videos from their heads. In my experience, they need encouragement as much as mechanics. If you only give them mechanical instruction, more often than not they'll get even more discouraged. Kind of like a bartender who pours you a drink but never listens to your problems.

When John approached me with the concept for this book, my first reaction was, "why me?" I'm not David Leadbetter or Butch Harmon, nobody wants to hear from me. But he wouldn't give up, and once we got going it was so much fun we couldn't stop. And the more he wrote, the more I began to believe that maybe I really did have something significant to contribute.

Lately there seems to be an undercurrent of seriousness to this game, like it's not okay to just go out and play. Maybe it's Tiger's hyper competitive nature that's setting the tone, I'm not sure. But the fact is, most people won't ever play competitive golf. Most people just want to go out with their buddies and play to the best of their ability, whatever that may be.

That's where this book can really help. Golf truly is a game for a lifetime, and this book will help you get the most out of every round, every hole, and every shot you play.

1
THE FORGET-ABOUT-IT GUIDE TO GOLF EQUIPMENT

"I've had some of the world's richest businessmen come for lessons. . . and the clubs they bought were the best that money could buy — but for someone else, not for them."

—TOMMY ARMOUR

The only thing more confusing than the golf swing is the technology that goes into modern golf equipment. Today we're bombarded with articles, ads and information on every little metallurgical marvel and every dimple deviation that comes along. Every four or five months there's something new. And the media covers anything and everything that relates to equipment advances. For 99 percent of the golfing public, it's just too much information.

You don't have to be a senior tour veteran to remember when the choices were a whole lot simpler. In irons you could choose pro-style blades or Ping Irons. Balls were Balata, and not Balata. Woods were wood, not some high-tech combination of five different space-age alloys. And shafts came in three different grades of steel: regular, stiff and super stiff.

Inevitably, technology is changing the game of golf, especially for the tour pros and the architects. But statistically speaking, all these marvelous new improvements are not helping our scores. (The average handicap in this country is still 16.1.) A ball's high-density polybutadiene core or ionomer transition layer might translate into a few more yards off the tee, but the element of doubt that's been introduced outweighs any distance advantage.

The rapid advances have only encouraged a lot more trial and error. And the minute you start experimenting with different shafts, testing new balls and researching drivers, doubt creeps in. Suddenly there's a little voice in the back of your mind all the time saying, "this ball's not right for me," or "this particular club's not forgiving enough," or "if only I had that 450cc driver, I could really crush it."

To play your best golf you just have to forget about it. You must have total confidence that the club in your hands is going to work as it was designed to. Otherwise, you'll subconsciously compensate. Instead of relying on one simple, dependable swing, you'll have to recall a different feeling for your long irons, your fairway woods and for your wedge. You'll start thinking that you have to change your swing to fit the club, and that's a very slippery slope.

So the question is, with all those choices and all those claims of product superiority, how do you know which clubs are right for you? How can you possibly sort through all the hype and make a confident buying decision? The answer is clubfitting.

MOST GOLF CLUBS FIT LIKE A CHEAP PAIR OF SOCKS.

Ever notice what a wide range of feet most socks will fit? It's quite common to find a pair of dress socks that "Fits men's sizes 7-12." Puh-lease. Those socks won't fit a guy with a size seven foot any better than the lucky guys on the other end of the scale. Socks are really only made for people with "average" size feet, like a nine or a ten.

The same thing can be said for most mass-marketed golf clubs. They're built to appeal to a wide range of players, but they really only fit a few.

Andy estimates that only 10 to 15 percent of all the students he has seen had clubs that were well fit. So when he gives a lesson, he always starts by doing a quick check of his student's equipment. He wants to know right away if it's the player's swing, or if it's the club that's producing the given ball flight.

If the clubs look good but the ball flight is sketchy, then there's some work to be done. But if the swing is sound and the ball flight stinks, it's an easy problem to fix... Just get the right club in the student's hands. And that's exactly what Andy does.

With a little trial and error any good clubfitter can produce a club that perfectly matches his student's swing and body type. And the results are impressive. You wouldn't believe how many people walk away thinking they just had the best lesson of their lives, when in reality it was simply a matter of having the right club for the swing they already had. It's a dramatic realization — that your existing swing, such as it is, can produce wonderful shots. Some people get irate when they see how simple it really is, and how much time and money they've wasted on standard clubs and lessons.

"Most players we teach are playing with equipment that is downright ill-suited to their needs."

-Bob Toski & Jim Flick

The fundamental problem with off-the-shelf clubs is this: If your clubs are not built to fit, you can make an absolutely perfect golf swing and still get crummy results. For instance, if the lie angle of your clubs is too flat, the ball will go right even when you make a perfect swing. Conversely, if the clubs are too upright, the ball will go left. This is a universal truth for golfers of all abilities. Now if you're Tiger Woods, you could quickly adjust to the discrepancy and play pretty well. But for most mortals it's just one more thing to have to worry about.

Think about how this misleading negative feedback affects the learning curve. If you're out on the range hitting hundreds of balls, and you're getting consistently poor results, what are you going to do? You're going to compensate. You're going to manipulate your swing in order to make the club produce the shot you want. It's only natural.

But in that case, your equipment is fooling you into thinking you need to change your swing, when you really need to change your equipment. In other words, the feedback you get from an ill-fitted club is not an accurate reflection of what's really happening with your golf swing. Most people see a bad result, and they assume it's a bad swing. But that's not necessarily the case.

Forget about it. Your clubs are supposed to reward a good swing just like good course architecture rewards good shots. So don't buy clubs just because they're popular. Invest in a set that truly fits your body type, your swing and your style of play. The custom-fitting process will eliminate any doubt you might have about your equipment and will ensure that you don't drop 1500 bucks on a set that's not right. It takes all the guesswork out of buying and gives you a huge advantage over your buddy who changes drivers more often than underwear.

WHY THE FAVORITE CLUB IN YOUR BAG IS THE FAVORITE CLUB IN YOUR BAG.

Almost every player, from beginner to tour pro, has a favorite club or two. Usually it's that tried and true 5-wood that's been in your bag forever, or an old, blade-style putter that your father gave you. Once you get your favorite club in your hand all the planets just seem to align themselves in your favor. Your confidence soars. Your swing comes together. And you can pull off shots that you'd never dream of trying with any other club.

Well guess what. There's a reason that one, magical club works so well, and it has nothing to do with the golf gods. It's probably the one club in your bag that fits. Just by dumb luck, it has the right shaft flex, the right kick point, the right lie angle, the right face design, the right swing weight and the right length. You're confident with it because it fits, or at least it's closer to the right fit than any of your other clubs.

But what about the other side of the coin? Just as we all have specific nemesis holes that continually give us fits, most people have a least one club in the bag that just doesn't seem to work. It's jinxed, or bent, or something.

> "If you buy a set of clubs off the shelf with no regard for lie angle, shaft flex, length or any other variables, you might get lucky and have one or two that actually fit you. Or you might not."
> **–Andy Heinly**

Obviously, part of the problem is a mental block that says, "I just can't hit this club." But what precipitates that is probably a fit issue. The shaft may be too stiff, or the kick point too low. Who knows? There are so many variables it's impossible to tell without doing a test with a certified clubfitter. But rest assured, it's not all in your head.

Unfortunately, very few players can differentiate between club problems and swing problems. Instead of realizing that it really could be the club, you assume it's a flaw in your swing and you act accordingly. Next thing you know, you start fiddling around with your mechanics in order to get good results with that one particular club, which in turn messes up the rest of your game. It's a vicious cycle that traps thousands of players every year.

Forget about it. Trying to recall and execute a different swing for one specific club is asking way too much. If you're hitting the ball pretty well and continue having trouble with one club, just get rid of it. It probably doesn't fit you, and forcing the issue will just ruin your confidence will all the other clubs in your bag.

The fact is, there's enough variation from one club to the next even within a set of name-brand irons to have a significant impact on your ball striking. You'll never hear this from a salesman, but it's true.

Graphite shafts are especially problematic. The manufacturing process is not perfect... there's going to be some variation, even among the shafts with the same flex rating and the same brand name. So it's up to the club manufacturer to test each shaft for consistency. However, quality control in many of the big companies consists of testing random samples from each batch of shafts, and things slip through the cracks. So you might end up with a seven iron that flexes differently than the eight, and so on.

Smaller companies that sell clubs exclusively through teaching professionals test every last shaft before they're shipped out. Plus, there's a follow-up appointment, where the clubfitter can double check the flex characteristics of each individual club. If something's amiss, he'll know it just by watching you hit balls.

And here's another thing about shaft manufacturing that's not common knowledge. There are no industry standards that define what the labels "stiff" or "regular" even mean. A lot of guys are convinced they need a stiff shaft — no doubt due to their immense power off the tee. But one company's "stiff" is the next company's "regular". Two stiff shafts can perform like polar opposites. There's no standardized testing.

Whenever Andy is asked about the stiffness of a club he's recommending, he always comes back with a flatteringly vague answer like, "yea, that's the shaft for you," or "Oh yea, I'm sure you can handle this one." Labels mean nothing. It's all about perception, and the perception is that if you're a good player, you should play with stiff clubs. Wrong.

How you buy clubs is more important than what clubs you buy.

Choosing a set of clubs these days can be a mind boggling affair. And a costly one at that. There are dozens of brands, hundreds of models and reams of information to sort through before you even set foot in a store.

Forget about it. If you want to simplify the process dramatically and take the guesswork out of buying clubs, start with a personalized clubfitting session. If you think in terms of fitting rather than buying, the shopping process will be downright fun and the decision will be easy.

Right off the bat you can rule out most of the big sporting goods chains and golf super stores. Their high volume approach to clubfitting is just a thinly veiled sales ploy. And don't even get us started on the level of expertise you can expect. There's nothing like listening to some kid trying to sell an 8 degree, 400 cc driver to an elderly woman who's lucky if she hits the ball 175 yards.

Instead, start by talking to the teaching pro at your club or favorite course. If he or she doesn't do clubfitting — and many will not — ask for a personal referral of someone who does. You can also go to the yellow pages and start calling some of the better courses in your area. Be specific that you're looking for comprehensive, on-course clubfitting services and find out what line or lines they carry.

There are many misconceptions as to what clubfitting really entails. Don't mistake arm measurements for a comprehensive club-fitting session. There's a lot more to it than your size. In fact, your size is relatively unimportant when you consider all the other variables. What we're talking about is a dynamic fitting process that involves a teacher and student on the driving range, experimenting with the club length, lie angle, loft and shaft flex until you find the precise combination that produces the optimal trajectory, distance and direction.

"If you buy a set of clubs from an experienced clubfitter to suit you and your swing, you will have increased your chances of playing to your potential. Good technique and correctly fitted clubs go hand in hand."
—David Leadbetter

Good clubfitting is a craft. It's part intuition, part science and a truly dynamic process that takes time, patience and a trained eye. No matter what the retail sales guys tell you, it can't be done in the confines of a store, and you sure can't do it on-line for $6.95, like some websites would lead you to believe. You also have to see the true flight of the ball in order to get a proper fit. Only the most so-phisticated new launch monitors can accurately portray ball flight.

The real beauty of the clubfitting process is that it eliminates doubt on the course and virtually guarantees you a good buy. Once the pro has gone through all the possible configurations and arrives at your precise specifications, you'll never have to think about it again. And confidence like that is a powerful tool to have. You'll never be standing on the tee second-guessing your decision. You won't be wondering if your driver's shaft is a little too stiff, or if you should have bought graphite shafts instead of steel. You'll know, in no uncertain terms, that your equipment is not keeping you from performing up to your potential.

Most people who have played for awhile embrace the concept of clubfitting, they just don't make it a high priority. There's always a "yeah, but" in the back of their mind… "Yeah, but clubfitting is too expensive." "Yeah, but isn't clubfitting for tour pros and scratch golfers." "Yeah, but I need to break 100 before I invest in something like that."

Forget about it. If you keep playing with clubs that are designed to accommodate a manufacturer's idea of the "average" golfer, it'll take you twice as long to reach your goal. If you do at all. You'll have a much better chance of reaching your potential with clubs that are built to your specifications, no matter what type of player your are. We contend that clubfitting actually has the biggest impact on inexperienced players. Tiger could probably break 80 playing with a pool cue, but most of us need a club that will make the game easier by eliminating any doubts about equipment. Especially if your style of play is wildly erratic.

Of course, for most people performance is not the only consideration when they're buying clubs. Money is also an issue, and many people forego custom clubs simply because of cost.

Actually, custom-made clubs are not that much more than a typical set of name-brand irons. Figure $110-$140 per club for the irons and $250-$450 for the woods.

Everybody likes to brag about the great bargains they got on their new clubs. But just because Scotland was the birthplace of the game doesn't mean you should be Scotch when it comes to equipment. Forget about it. Bargain-basement clubs, more often than not, will produce bargain-basement results. And before you know it you'll be back in the market again searching for the something better. It will be cheaper in the long run just to invest in custom clubs to begin with.

You should also be careful not to spend too much on any given club. The problem is, if you spend $600 on a new driver right off the shelf you'll have a lot of motivation to make it work, no matter how wild you are with it. No one wants to admit they made a bad purchase, and you'd be amazed how long some people will continue to play a club even if they can't really hit it from day one. Luckily, you won't have to worry about that if you go through the clubfitting process.

Another nice thing about custom clubs is that you don't pay for a 2-iron you're never going to use. There's no such thing as a "set" of clubs anymore, anyway. There are only individual tools you use for different course situations. Look in the bag of the typical LPGA pro these days and you'll usually see five different woods, four wedges and no numbers lower than a 5 in the iron department. The macho days of the 1-iron, it seems, are gone for good.

Andy would rather see a player with six well-fit clubs, rather than a hodge-podge of 14 ill-fitting ones. Again, he likes to keep things simple. Besides, most people who are learning the game have very little distance control. They hit their 5-iron the same as their 8, which goes about as far as their pitching wedge. So you don't need all the choices. Better to be proficient with a few, than wild with the whole lot of them.

If you play a lot of newer courses you might need a lob wedge. But not until you can handle a normal sand wedge with confidence. Again, that's the beauty of having a clubfitting professional watching you hit balls. He'll know if you're not ready for that 60-degree wedge or that oversized driver, and he won't stick you with a club you can't handle.

When I lived in Portland, Oregon, my Cobra Baffler 4-wood was my favorite club. An updated version of the old persimmon classic, it had a small clubhead and deep rails on the bottom. It was the perfect tool for hitting balls out of rough that's soggier than discount swampland. Didn't matter how deep or wet it was; the ball would come rocketing out of there, dead straight almost every time.

Then I moved to Central Oregon, where the air is thin and the grass is dormant four months out of the year. For the first time I was playing on tightly cut, bentgrass fairways with immaculately trimmed one-inch rough. And also for the first time, my dependable old Baffler began to let me down. I couldn't figure it out. With each bad shot my confidence was beaten down a little more until I couldn't stand over the ball with that club in my hand. I had to put it away for good.

Needless to say, not being able to hit my favorite club affected my entire game. I even started fiddling with my swing to compensate for it.

But it wasn't me, it was the club. It just wasn't made for the new course conditions I was facing. There wasn't any thick, wet rough to dig the ball out of, and those rails made it really hard to hit anything off tightly cropped fairways. It simply wasn't the right tool for the job.

Clubfitting and building has evolved into quite a science. They can analyze your launch angle and the ball's spin rate. They can choose from a thousand different graphite composite shafts with varying degrees of flex and different kick points. They can even use metal alloys in clubheads that perform too darn well for the USGA. Luckily, there are people out there who make a career out of understanding all of it so we don't have to. Just find a good clubfitter and forget about it.

Of all the sure-fire ways to improve your golf game, nothing comes close to a good clubfitting session. There's not a video, book or training aid in the world that can produce more dramatic results in less time than simply finding the right set of clubs for your unique swing. Once you go through the process you'll never go back to off-the-shelf clubs again.

IGNORE WHO PLAYS WHAT ON TOUR, AND FORGET ABOUT THE HAND-ME-DOWNS.

If you're a statistics nut you'll love the PGA's official website. They have esoteric data on every conceivable aspect of the game, including who plays what clubs. Forget about it. Don't even go there.

There is no correlation between those PGA tour statistics and the performance of the clubs you can buy in the store. The tour pros are sticklers when it comes to equipment... there's not a player out there who didn't have his clubs custom fit to the Nth degree. So even if you buy the same brand and the same model, you won't be playing the same club.

We can't emphasize this enough: You cannot buy the same clubs the pros use, but you can go through the same clubfitting process. So what does it matter if more pros play Mizuno irons, or if the longest driver on tour happens to be Taylor Made. It means nothing to those guys, so why should it matter to you?

"It's easy to jump on the bandwagon and go with whatever your favorite pro is using. It might even give your confidence a shot in the arm. For awhile. Eventually, though, the euphoria wears off."
                                                                    -Dave Pelz

If you're honest about it you'll admit it has more to do with keeping up with the Joneses than keeping your scores down. The truth is, peer pressure and ego dictate more club purchases than anything else. If you're consistently getting outdriven, it's awfully tempting to try something new. Anything that will give you a few extra yards.

Forget about it. Let them brag all day long about their hot new driver with the super high COR rating. Gimmicks will mean nothing to you when you have the confidence that a good clubfitting session produces. Let your game do the talking... once you start winning all the money in your friendly foursome the rest of the guys will be looking to you for equipment advice.

Harvey Penick, the old sage who coached Ben Crenshaw and Tom Kite, once said that the biggest problem with women golfers is their husbands. Husbands who provide hand-me-down clubs and uninformed instruction.

You've probably seen this before: The loving husband wants his wife to take up the game, but they don't really want to invest a lot of money until she knows she likes the sport. So he spends 1,200 bucks on a new set of clubs for himself and takes his old, hand-me-down set and has the shafts cut down to size for his wife.

"Sure, just lop off a few inches, put on some new grips and they'll be perfect for her," he says. Nothing could be further from the truth.

Women, almost universally, have a hard time generating sufficient clubhead speed. What they need is a soft, flexible shaft that will help whip the clubhead through impact — exactly the opposite of what you get from a cut-down club of any kind.

It doesn't matter how nice that set of irons was to start with, they're not going to work for her unless they're completely reshafted and rebuilt specifically for her. And even then, there are limits to what a good clubmaker can do. You might as well make her play left handed with one eye closed. She's not going to get your old 3-iron airborne. And when you combine the jury-rigged equipment with the pressure filled "lessons" she gets from her spouse, she's doomed to failure. There's no way she's going to enjoy the game.

Same thing goes for your kids. Don't waste their time with sticks that are more suited to a strong male player. Invest in a good set of properly fitted clubs from the very beginning. There are some great junior sets on the market now that have the whippiest little shafts you've ever seen. They're great confidence boosters.

And for Pete's sake, forget about trying to teach them yourself. If your spouse is taking up the game get her some private lessons from someone who knows a lot more about the game than you do. It's the better part of valor. If it's your kids, just take them out and let them have some fun. Plunking balls into the water hazards is always a hit. Whiffle balls in the back yard. Putt-putt. Anything but the serious rounds that most adults insist upon.

There's no doubt that the advances in club design and ball construction are exciting. Who wouldn't like to hit a 350 yard drive? But don't let all the talk about technology distract you. Don't get too caught-up in the marketing hype. No matter what the clubs are made of, it still comes down to this: Do they work for you, or against you? Are the clubs suited to your style and your swing, or are they really designed for someone else? When you make a good swing, will the club reward you, or let you down?

2
THE FORGET-ABOUT-IT GUIDE TO LEARNING

"Once in a while I imagine stepping into the mind of a hacker trying to figure out the game without any help from a good teaching pro. I don't stay long, because it's like stumbling through the fun house at an amusement park — it's full of false paths and bumpy tracks and flashing signs and trick mirrors and muffled screams and all kinds of surprises popping out and attacking you."

—Sam Snead

There's a lot to learn about the game of golf. If you're so inclined, you could spend a lifetime studying the rich history of the game, the players, the architecture and of course, the swing. Unfortunately, in this game learning does not translate into performance.

In fact, for many people the more they learn about the game the harder it gets.

Kids will always remind you how how simple this game can be: Just hold the club like this and hit the ball. Kids don't waste their time trying to figure out "how," they just "do." And they seem to get such joy out of it. Just watching the ball fly through the air is reward enough.

Adults, on the other hand, always need to know why, how and what-for. We complicate things by trying to learn all the ins and outs of the swing when really all we need to know is the feeling of hitting the ball at the target. A lot of players are so busy analyzing the cause and effect, they lose sight of the real goal... to get the ball in the hole, and have fun in the process.

When it comes to learning golf, less is more. Less input. Less thinking. Less analysis. We don't believe you have to break down your entire swing in order to improve your game. In fact, for 90 percent of you, the harder you try to "understand" your swing, the harder the game will get.

Percy Boomer said it well, almost 70 years ago: "Do not try too hard to understand with your mind... You play golf by feeling, not by scientific analysis."

Golf is a game of hope and potential. No matter how bad things get, there's always the potential for a good shot or a good hole or a good round just down the road. The problem with this eternal optimism is that it fools us into thinking we can find the answer to all our golf problems in an instructional video or book or magazine. It fuels our thirst for knowledge and blinds us to the most important fact of golf life... That the more we learn, the harder the game gets. The more noise there is in your head, the less likely your body is to perform in a consistent, trained manner.

When Ernie Els won the British Open in 2002, he attributed much of his success to his new approach to the mental game. Even though he slipped up (some would say choked) and was forced into a playoff, he said he was able to silence the voices in his head and just trust himself.

Unfortunately, the usual modus operandi of the avid American golfer is just the opposite. Once we're bitten by the curse of the golf bug, we start reading articles, listening to friends and watching the pros on TV. We buy training aids for three easy payments of only $29.95. We listen to tapes and look at statistics. We study high-speed video images of picture-perfect pros in order to pinpoint our swing faults. We fill our heads with all the information we can get, and then we go out and pound balls. Tons and tons of balls every year. The driving range phenomenon is so pervasive I'm betting it's going to be the next big fitness trend.

Forget about it. Trying to teach yourself the game that way is like self-administering prescription medicine without getting any sort of diagnosis from a doctor. "Let's see if this Valium will help my tempo this week!"

In the 1906 classic, *Swing The Clubhead*, Ernest Jones used the analogy of an alley cat, "picking up scraps of the food of golf as you go along." Andy and I call it the binge and purge school of golf. You gorge on information of all different flavors, from dozens of different sources. You fill up on the latest tidbits from big name golf gurus. You analyze your swing and experiment with just about every new method that comes along. Then you try to apply your newfound knowledge to your own swing.

Problem is, it's virtually impossible to learn even the most basic fundamentals without being exposed to tons of conflicting information. And when that hot new tip doesn't work, you have to throw it out and start all over again with another approach. Binge and purge, binge and purge. It's a treadmill of learning and un-learning that seldom results in any real, long-term improvement. In fact, it usually leads to utter confusion and frustration. In some cases, it's even enough to drive people away from the game.

Forget about it. As Percy Boomer once said, the self-taught golfer is a poorly taught one. You see, golf is not a game of knowledge, it's a game of skill. You can't just learn the theories of the swing, you have to develop the skills you need to play the game.

So the question is, how do you do that? How can you develop those skills? How can you learn to have fun playing the game without getting bogged down in the mechanics of the swing? How can you simplify the learning process and lower your scores at the same time?

First of all, you have to accept the fact that learning is a process. A life-long process, in fact. No matter how studious or naturally athletic you are, golf is not something you just pick up. It's not going to happen overnight and there is no secret to the game hiding in some instructional video somewhere.

Second, you need a systematic approach to learning the game that is tailored to your individual preferences and psychological make-up. We're not talking about a Hogan-like habit of hitting 700 balls day, we're talking about a systematic learning program that focuses not on mechanics but on play. It should be a fun, fulfilling routine that is built on a foundation of basic knowledge, sound fundamentals, expert coaching, and focused practice. Yes, practice.

Finally, you need a professional to oversee the whole learning process. A good pro will break it down into manageable chunks and guide you gently through the acquisition of skills without overwhelming you with information.

If you try to go it alone, the learning process will inevitably turn into an endless cycle of experimentation, confusion and frustration. One magazine tells you this is the best way to cure a slice and another magazine tells you something completely different. Every month there's a new method or a hot new trend on tour to side-track your learning efforts. Even the pros have a hard time sorting through all the instructional information that's out there. The average person can't possibly know which method to use, or which tips will hurt more than they'll help. Without any guidance you won't know if you're doing things right or just getting lucky.

KNOWING IS EASY. IT'S LEARNING THAT'S TOUGH.

There's a saying in the publishing industry that goes something like this: "People who read how-to books want to know, but they don't want to learn." Learning just involves too much work. This is particularly true for those of us who are searching for the ultimate answer to all our golfing woes. We want to know the secret to those 300-yard drives, but we're too impatient to go through the learning process required to develop that highly sought-after skill.

As any college student will attest, there's a big difference between knowing and learning. Knowing is easy. You can know all the answers for a multiple choice test without learning a thing.

In golf — as in life — knowledge alone won't get you very far. For instance, there are millions of people out there who know an open clubface will produce a slice. They probably even know some sure-fire drills that would cure the problem. And still, year after year, they keep hitting the big chaquita way right. They simply haven't *learned* how to apply that information to their own swing. They haven't made the leap from knowing to doing.

> "The right way of learning golf has almost nothing in common with the learning we did in school. It's an entirely different process. What you need to learn or memorize are not the technical or mathematical details of a good shot, but the feel of it."
>
> **– Percy Boomer**

In his book *Rethinking Golf*, Chuck Hogan makes an interesting distinction between information and knowledge. He says "we're drowning in information while starving for knowledge." But even that isn't enough. Knowledge is nice to have, but it's useless on the golf course until you can do something with it. Knowledge must be translated into a skill, and skill into habit. It has to be ingrained so well that you can forget about it completely and still be able to call it up without thinking. It's not really learned until it's as mindless as breathing.

Again, in this game there is very little connection between knowledge and performance. So if you really want to learn the game you have to forget about *knowing* and start *doing*. Stop filling your head, and start training your body.

FORGET ABOUT LEARNING "THE SWING." LEARN TO PLAY YOUR OWN SHOTS.

Let's get this perfectly straight. Everyone talks about the golf swing like it's a proper noun. Like there's one, idealistic model of efficiency that everyone should emulate. There isn't. Swing is a verb. It's something you do, not something you have. And every golfer does it a little differently.

Everybody makes fun of the way Jim Furyk swings, but it worked well enough to win the U.S. Open. Arnold Palmer's swing was never a thing of beauty. Neither was Lee Trevino's, but they knew how to play the shots they needed to play. They weren't overly concerned with the process — how to get it there — they just got it there. In the fairway. On the green. Close to the flag. And in the hole.

There's a big difference between learning to play golf, and learning the golf swing. There's no need to do both. Forget about it. The more you learn about the golf swing, the more difficult the game will get. There are just too many theories. Too many methods. And too much contradictory information out there.

The fact is, you don't have to understand all the technicalities of the golf swing in order to play well. You can get the feel of a new swing without understanding why it works. You don't need a textbook swing to kick the pants off everyone in your men's club.

Look at Bruce Leitzke. Here's a guy who virtually never practices his swing. He just goes out there and plays. He makes his natural swing — a power fade — work for him, and he never, ever messes with it. His low-maintenance approach earned him 13 wins on the regular tour and puts him in the top 15 on the all-time money list. Now he's winning regularly on the Champion's tour.

If you stay focused on learning golf shots, rather than the golf swing, you'll save yourself a lot of time and trouble. If you're fairly new to the game it's best to start out on the practice green. Learn to putt, then move up to the chip shot. Once you've developed a good feel for those, you can take that skill and apply it to some pitch shots and short iron approaches. Then, and only then, should you be hitting full shots at the driving range. (More on how to practice efficiently in Chapter 4.)

ALL THE TIPS, HINTS AND TIDBITS ARE TOTALLY OUT OF CONTEXT.

All the tips you read in magazines or see on the Golf Channel are valid for someone. There's a lot of good information out there, but it may not have any relevance to your particular problem. What's missing is the meaningful context of your own swing, your own game, and your own personal approach to learning.

And here's the rub. It takes a very astute student of the golf swing to understand the impact that a simple change can have within the context of your unique game. It's very difficult to answer the question, "yea, but what's that mean for me?"

"Tips which are guaranteed to improve your game are easy enough to come by. Every clubhouse is full of them. But all this advice is dangerous... Anyone who takes too much advice from too many different sources will be baffled and confused by the opposite theories and contradictory practices of acknowledged masters."
- Percy Boomer

You've heard the saying, "for every action, there is an equal and opposite reaction." Well in golf, that means every little adjustment you make in your swing causes a chain reaction. The minute you master that new little technique you picked up from a friend, at least one other fault rears its ugly head. So then you search for the solution to the new fault, and round and round you go. It's like a treadmill of learning misery.

So forget about it! Don't even go there. Instead, let a good teaching pro do the thinking for you.

A good instructor will understand all the underlying technical issues, and if he's any good he'll translate them into a few simple solutions. He'll see the problem, and he'll understand all the technical implications of your faults, but he won't dwell on them. He'll stay focused on the positive, big-picture issues.

He'll screen out the million and one things that you don't need to fix, and help you apply positive changes within the context of your own game, your own physical limitations and your own learning style.

Instead of just treating the symptoms, like a weak slice or a screaming hook, a good pro will quickly treat the root of the problem. The cancer, if you will. Instead of taking a band-aid approach he'll weed out the thousands of irrelevant tips and give you something to work on that, with some consistent practice, will cure the real ailment. He will limit you to only the tips that relate to your unique swing.

One of the leading golf publications recently ran an article that included a tip from each of the top 50 instructors in the country. There's the goal-post drill, the frying-pan drill, the popcorn drill. One tells you to "catch the plane," another to "stop, drop and roll." If you listen to even one-tenth of these tips you'll be so confused you won't know which way's up. And these are the best instructors in the country! Imagine how misguided the tips are that come from your friends and golfing acquaintances.

Forget about it. Don't listen to them. The next time someone offers unsolicited advice, just smile and say thanks, but no thanks.

YOUR PERCEPTION ISN'T EVEN CLOSE TO REALITY.

The second fundamental problem with the binge and purge approach to learning is perception. The fact is, there's a big difference between what you think you're doing with your swing and what you're really doing. That's why self-analysis and self-diagnosis seldom works. Because it only feels like you're doing things "right."

Forget about it. Your senses are not as accurate as you'd like to believe. Perception is not reality. Even if you work with a mirror or a video camera you'll still have a skewed perception of your own golf swing. It's like hearing yourself on the radio. You know it's you, but you'd swear it doesn't sound anything at all like you.

"As for learning by observation... unfortunately that which the adult onlooker sees is not sensed in the same way by the performer. One uses his sense of sight, the other his sense of feel."
                                                    – Ernest Jones

Think about how this affects long-term learning: Let's say you find a tip that you're determined to incorporate into your swing. Naturally, you head to the driving range and practice it over and over and over again until you think you've got it. But how do you really know unless you have some objective feedback? What happens if you think you're doing it right, but you're still not seeing the results you want? Most likely you'll jump to the conclusion that the tip doesn't work and move on to some other theory. It's a vicious circle. You binge on tips that may not even apply to you and then you have trouble purging that information from your memory.

Forget about it! There's no such thing as un-learning. You don't forget old habits, you can only replace old habits with new ones. So if you want to avoid that learning trap quit binging on all those magazine articles. Sell all your instruction videos on ebay and get with a good teaching pro.

There aren't many self-taught scratch golfers out there, but there are a lot of self-taught hackers who've been playing for 35 years without ever breaking 90. And you'd be amazed at how many of them claim to "know their swing." Even the best golfers in the world need an outside perspective from time to time.

If anybody understands the idiosyncrasies of his own golf swing, it's Tiger Woods. His awareness is legendary. When he arrived at Andy's club for the 1996 U.S. Amateur, he was working with Butch Harmon on just one simple aspect of his swing. Nothing else. Then in 1999 — when Tiger needed to make a more significant change in his swing — he again turned to Butch Harmon for guidance. The results, of course, speak for themselves.

A good instructor will help you develop awareness of your own. Awareness of what the clubhead is doing, awareness of the target and awareness of your set-up is crucial to learning. In fact, Timothy Gallwey in *The Inner Game of Golf* says, without awareness there is no such thing as learning… "Whatever increases the quality of awareness in an individual also increases the quality of learning, performance and enjoyment."

If your perception is skewed by a lack of awareness, it follows that if you improve awareness you'll also improve your perception of what's going on. At the very least you'll see how skewed your perception really is. And that, by itself, is much more productive than learning about the swing of Ben Hogan, Ernie Els or any other top pro.

So forget about what everyone else is doing. Stop poring over those sequential, high-speed photos of the pros, and start focusing on how your own swing feels. Get tuned-in to the different sensations that come from all your shots, good and bad. Then you'll be on your way to real improvement.

THERE'S NOTHING POSITIVE ABOUT ALL THE NEGATIVE THINKING.

Remember Dr. Ruth Westheimer? She had a talk radio program back in the '80s where she answered every call with, "Hi you're on zee air. Vhat's your problem?"

Golf instruction is like that. Rather than taking a positive approach — and focusing on the pleasure of the game — everyone wants to zero in on specific performance problems. Whether you're learning on your own, or with an instructor, beware of this backward approach that starts with your faults and then, eventually, gets around to the appropriate fixes.

Don't waste your time with "How Not To" articles: How not to three-putt. How not to slice. How not to move your head. Don't do this, don't do that. That kind of instruction is based on the theory that if you understand the technicalities of what you're doing wrong, you'll eventually be able to do it right. One big-name guru takes it even farther, claiming that confusion opens the door to discovery.

No, confusion only leads to frustration — and prosperity for golf pros who live off frustrated students. Confusion is the only thing you can count on if you're trying to learn the game from books, videos and friendly tips from your uncle Harry.

Forget about it. You'll always have faults in your swing and focusing on the negatives will just make matters worse. What you want is a positive approach to learning. Instead of practicing things that will help you avoid bad swings, practice the fundamental behaviors that will produce good, accurate shots. Don't try to correct the problem from the previous shot, just observe the results and forget about it. Then approach the next shot in a positive frame of mind using a routine that you know will produce good results.

> "Most of the teaching of golf is completely negative – and a purely negative thing can have no positive value. We can all find faults in each other's game, millions of them, and we all start off by pointing out these faults and curing them."
>
> **– Percy Boomer**

Sports psychologists have been preaching positive thinking for years. But you can't just turn it on when you're on the course. You have to practice it. The tendency on the driving range is to hit and correct, hit and correct. But if you're fixating on negatives during practice, it's going to be almost impossible to shift into a positive mode on the first tee.

A negative approach to learning also compounds the perception problem. In order to benefit from the "fixes" you find in most books, you must have an accurate read on what your faults really are. Unfortunately, most people are assuming they have the same problem as the guy in the book because they're getting the same results. But a slice, for instance, can have many different causes.

The monthly golf publications are famous for their quick fix articles based on the average golfer's most common faults. It's ironic though, when they juxtapose that editorial slant with advice on the mental game from renowned sports psychologists. The latter will tell you it's all about visualizing the ideal shot and maintaining a positive mental attitude. But just in case, here's an article with all the technical advice you'll ever need for those easy little chips.

Most golf instruction is conducted in a "do this, do that" manner. While that's better than a "don't do that" approach, it still has pitfalls. Timothy Gallwey calls it "Do" instruction and defines it as an order from the mind of the teacher to the body of the student. Needless to say, there's a lot that gets lost in translation.

Instead of telling a student what he should do, which implies he's doing something he shouldn't, Gallwey suggests a softer approach. Instead of saying "you need to hit it more from inside to out" it would go like this: "See if you can feel which way the clubhead is traveling through the ball right now." Simply focus your awareness on it. It's an exercise that will produce dramatic results.

As Gallwey says, "do" instruction asks the golfer to achieve a certain result that he may not feel he can produce. "Awareness instruction, on the other hand, asks only one thing of the conscious mind: pay attention to what is happening." It's a radically different frame of reference that's focused on what is happening, rather than what should be happening.

Andy often uses simple training aids and drills that help improve awareness without employing any analysis. Rather than just telling students how, he enables them to feel how to do something without thinking about how to do it. He calls them no-brainer trainers, and I can attest to their effectiveness.

So forget about acquiring all sorts of knowledge. Instead, try the inner game approach and work on improving awareness. Awareness is much more practical than knowledge. Awareness is feel-oriented, knowledge is information oriented. Awareness has a direct connection to performance. Knowledge doesn't. And awareness increases our ability to stay focused and in the moment. Knowledge is just a distraction.

ARTIST OR ROCKET SCIENTIST? HOW YOUR MENTAL MAKE-UP AFFECTS LEARNING.

When I was younger, I didn't think much about my self-made golf swing. My practice regime usually involved whiffle ball tournaments in the yard or an occasional round of putt-putt. On the course I was a hooker and a scrambler. Seve Ballesteros was my hero and I spent so much time in the trees I once considered becoming a forestry major. Like most 20-something kids, I never even considered laying up off the tee.

Then, when I got "serious" about the game and started playing in some club events, my style began to evolve. Slowly but surely I started getting more conservative. Instead of ripping it down there and taking my chances with my scrambling ability, I started calculating the risks. Laying up. Whimping out. At the time, I thought I was playing smart because that's what all the golf magazines said to do. But when I look back on it, I was actually stifling the best thing I had going for me... my creativity.

See, I'm a creative, right-brained kinda guy. I'm not inclined to science and engineering, but when it came to golf, that's exactly the approach I thought I had to use. So I started analyzing my swing, fiddling with my putting, and practicing all the wrong things. It worked alright for about one season, but in the long run it was a recipe for disaster. The approach eventually manifested itself as a weak slice, which I'd never experienced in my entire life, and a debilitating case of the yips. The only approach to learning the game that I'd ever heard of was not even remotely suited to my personality. My brain's just not wired that way.

> "What you are teaching is like the food you eat. First it must be swallowed. Then it must be digested. But it does no good until it has been assimilated."
> **- Earnest Jones**

The official PGA teaching manual mentions four different learning styles. Good teaching pros like Andy will recognize your style within the first few minutes of a lesson. But you also have to consider your left-brained or right-brained tendencies.

There's a good book on the subject called *How To Learn Anything Quickly*. It will help you identify your tendencies in order to improve your chances of learning more efficiently. Once you've pinpointed your own style, you can choose the best learning environment and the right instructor. Then you can create a training program that's best suited to your personality and your individual goals. Here's a quick run-down of the basic styles:

Some lucky people are visual learners. They see a demonstration and they can do it, just like that. In golf, this takes tremendous body awareness. Visual people are very organized and have an affinity for charts and graphs. As long as the information is presented in a logical, step-by-step format left-brained visual learners have the best chance of learning golf through books and magazines. If everyone had visual, left-brained orientation we'd never be writing this book.

Auditory people, on the other hand, learn by listening, hearing and discussing things. It's the left-brained auditory types who spend countless hours on the driving range discussing the minutia of the swing. The sound of a solid hit is a great learning tool especially for right-brained auditory people.

Tactile learners connect with a lesson by using their hands and by perceiving sensations. They have an extra-perceptive sense of touch and may have a natural feel for the game. However, right-brained tactile people get bogged down easily in details, preferring instead a more intuitive approach.

Kinesthetic people learn by doing — by using their large motor skills and by getting actively involved through simulations, role-playing and experimentation. They're usually pretty coordinated, but they can't sit still through a lecture. Kinesthetic, right brained people need an unstructured, imaginative and free-flowing approach to instruction. As any grade school teacher will tell you, many boys are kinesthetic learners. Lessons just won't sink in unless they can touch something, interact with other kids, and generally engage their whole being in the problem.

Left brain, right brain. Tactile or audio. The point is, 99 percent of all golf instruction methods and materials are designed, unwittingly, for left- brained visually-oriented people. If you don't fit into that tidy little category, you have to find a better approach than just reading books. And even if you do fit neatly into that category, you'll need to get out of your comfort zone if you want to play well on the course.

Golf Digest once did a study on the brain-wave activity while playing golf and concluded that in order to play well you have to engage the right side of your brain, while trying to quell the buzz of activity in the left side where all those technical swing thoughts come from.

Very few instructors are in tune with this. They don't know how to teach creativity or imaginative shot making, they only know how to correct mechanical mistakes. For people like me, who are tactile or kinesthetic right-brained learners, that approach just doesn't work. I'm better off hitting a whiffle ball around with my 8-year-old son.

As Sam Snead once said, "The more the mind breaks down the swing intellectually, the more often your nerves break down trying to put it into action."

So figure out what your personal learning style is, and take advantage of it. If you're kinesthetic and right brained, don't let anyone clog your head with an in-depth discussion of why your right arm position isn't "right" or why you shouldn't do something. Just smile and say excuse me.

If you're left brained and visually oriented, consider yourself lucky. All those instruction manuals are written just for you. But that means you're even more susceptible to the binge and purge syndrome. And remember, you may be able to learn some new techniques by using a rocket-scientist approach, but very, very few people can perform well on the course if they're stuck in that left-brained frame of mind.

SO MANY METHODS, SO LITTLE TIME.

Just about every month there's a new method out there. That's how they sell magazines. In fact, there are almost as many methods out there as there are teaching pros, and many are completely contradictory to one another.

One method advocates the use of the legs and hips in the swing. Another focuses only on the "big" muscles, as if you have any of those. Yet another emphasizes the role of the hands and the leverage created by the geometric angles of arms and shaft. There's an eight-step swing and a 10-step swing. There's the Y factor, the K factor and my personal favorite, the Z factor. There's gravity golf and natural golf. Unfortunately, after you experiment with all these methods, all you're left with is "seismic" golf, where you're so completely rattled you can't stand over a simple sand wedge shot without being seized by incurable shanks.

Forget about it. There is no right method for swinging a golf club, and bouncing from one method to another is a sure-fire way to maintain your current level of mediocrity. We could even argue that all methods are misguided.

By definition, a method is complicated and task-oriented. It implies a step-by-step breakdown of the swing involving organization, classification and categorization. Methods focus on the process of building "a swing" rather than the results produced by the swing.

Maybe a better word would be an "approach." Approach is more general. More mental than physical. And it doesn't imply such finality. An approach can be tweaked and molded to fit different people, while methods are rigid and unforgiving. You either buy-in wholeheartedly or you go on to something else.

Better yet, why not call it a "style." Sam Snead had style. Arnold Palmer had style. Sergio Garcia has style. Most of the other young guys on tour have methods.

> **"I'm afraid I've seen too many methods come and go in my half century in golf to really believe that the latest method on the market, whatever it may be, is going to solve anybody's golf problems for long."**
> **– Sam Snead**

So forget about the latest methods and focus on developing a style of play that reflects who you really are, rather than who looks good in sequential swing photographs. Quit judging the swing, and start gauging everything by where the ball ends up.

3
THE FORGET-ABOUT-IT GUIDE TO TAKING LESSONS

"The fault with much of the golf teaching of today is that the teacher tries to eradicate specific faults by issuing specific instructions. In short, the good tip system again. This is fatal, mainly because it is no system at all but just a conglomeration of golf patent medicines. I do not believe that any instruction that is not part of a consistent system can be of any permanent benefit."

—PERCY BOOMER

Get this. There's a writer out there who's on a quest to take a lesson from every one of the top 100 golf instructors in the country. He admits he has a problem. But hey, it makes great material, and who would pass up an all-expense paid trip to the finest golf schools in the country?

Actually, I would. Unless the assignment was to document the damage to my game, I would have to say thanks, but no thanks. That's not to say the gurus couldn't improve my swing. On the contrary. It's just that for me, more lessons on swing mechanics are not going to get me anywhere. Given my goals, my skill level, and my personality, that kind of instruction will do me more harm than good.

I've had eight lessons from six different instructors, not including the lessons I took when I was 12. And I have to admit, none of my teachers ever appeared on that top 100 list.

The first of those lessons was about as memorable as a really bad movie. I recall nothing of it, except that I was on the driving range at night with someone who was telling me something that must have had some relevance to someone's golf swing at some point in history. But it didn't have anything to do with my game.

Another unproductive lesson was with a young assistant pro who couldn't teach a rat to take cheese. Oh, he talked a good game — and the information was interesting enough — but there was nothing that I could apply. Nothing but good theories and hypothetical fixes. Maybe it was my state of mind that day, but everything about that lesson seemed wrong. Not just contrary to what I already knew, or counter productive, but wrong in anybody's book.

One lesson that I found rather engaging — in a twisted sort of way — involved a former PGA tour winner, an indoor hitting cage and a theory that went something like this: Before you can learn to hit it straight, you have to learn to hit it right to left and left to right. So instead of a dependable draw with the occasional

THE FORGET-ABOUT-IT GUIDE TO TAKING LESSONS

THE FORGET-ABOUT-IT GUIDE TO TAKING LESSONS   51

push to the right, I came out of that lesson with two entirely new shots: the Top-Gun style pull-hook and the weak, banana ball. I give the guy credit. To this day, I can work the ball around a tree in either direction. Hitting it straight must have been covered in the second lesson, which I never got around to taking.

When the video camera first appeared on the driving ranges of America I was totally hip to it. I scouted a good location, plotted the best time of day for good, natural light, set up my camera on a tripod and then filmed my swing from every angle you can imagine. The only thing missing from the production was a crane cam for the birds-eye view of my swing.

Since the camera couldn't pick-up the ball's flight, I'd hit a shot, watch the results and turn to the camera and do a little commentary. "That was a little thin, 10 yards right." Or "crushed that one, but held on and left the clubface open." "Ooops, slid my hips, then tried to compensate by slapping my hands through at the last second producing a top-spin pull hook that sailed 40 yards left nearly missing that foursome on the 18th tee." I had all the shots.

Funny thing was, they all looked good to me on tape. Despite the slow-motion technology and the freeze-frame function, I just couldn't see the subtleties that were causing my lousy shots. If it weren't for the running narration I would have sworn every shot sailed straight at the hole.

So I decided to find a pro who could do a more thorough video analysis. Yea, just what I needed. More detail. In my first official video lesson the instructor taped my swing and then diagrammed all the angles and positions from the set-up to the finish. Spine angle. Hips. Shoulders. Angle of the right arm at the top. You name it, we looked at it. Then, just for a comparison, he super-imposed Ernie Els onto the screen. Boy, what a low blow. Just when I thought I was doing a lot of things pretty well, he throws The Big Easy at me. I didn't look anything like him, and I came away more confused and depressed than ever.

Needless to say, none of these lessons resulted in any im-provement in my net scores. The take-away, for me, was I might as well just teach myself.

Then, during the summer of 2002, I had my first lesson with Andy Heinly. In less than an hour Andy did more for my game than all the other instructors put together. His no-nonsense approach, and the way he communicated the simplicity of the game, was an epiphany for me.

We started by simply talking about my game. Not my swing, but my game. Where I've been, where I want to be and why I play. Then Andy watched patiently, silently, while I forced a few balls into the air with my 7-iron. (Most of the shots were a little bit thin and a little short of the target, just like my previous golf lessons.) Without a word, Andy went to his giant golf bag of tricks and pulled out a fun little training aid that I had never seen — a yellow plastic ball, about the size of a whiffle ball, attached by a small rope to the grip of a golf club. (It's a modern version of Ernest Jones' classic pen knife on the end of a handkerchief.) Andy took the contraption and started swinging the feather-weight ball back and forth with an effortless whoosh forward and another whoosh back. It looked like child's play.

"Swing this a few times," he said.

To my utter horror I couldn't do it. On my first several attempts the ball didn't whoosh around in big, beautiful arc as it did for Andy. It fell and bounced and caromed off me as I tried to muscle the stupid little toy through my full swing. I didn't have the rhythm. I didn't have the feel. I didn't have the coordination of a four-month old St. Bernard.

"Just relax your arms," he said.

I kinda laughed and tried again with a lot less effort. Still no luck. Swinging the thing was easy enough, but keeping the rope taught was a true test of skill and trust. I felt stupid and Andy wasn't offering any sure-fire advice. So I stopped, shook my arms out and focused on feeling the ball at the end of the rope. Just let it flow. Let gravity do the work. Be the ball. Finally, the string started to tighten and the ball began to behave. No whooshing sound yet, but I had it moving back and forth with some consistency. All the pieces of my swing started to sync into one, coherent motion.

"There you go," Andy says. "Now I want to hear it."

I picked up the tempo a smidge. Loose as a goose now, I could hear the ball whooshing through the swing, building to a crescendo at just the right spot... past the normal impact point. Ah-ha. At that moment I realized what Ernest Jones was talking about all those years ago when he said you must swing the clubhead. It sounds like such a no-brainer, but when you replace the clubhead with a whiffle ball it's not so simple. Not by a long shot.

Once I had the feel for that toy, we moved on to half-swings with an 8-iron. Making the exact same motion, I focused only on feeling the clubhead swinging back and forth and back and forth with no effort whatsoever. There were no thoughts of a full shoulder turn, a reverse pivot or a proper spine angle. Just clubhead and target. Clubhead and target.

Then Andy put a ball down in front of me, and without missing a beat I caught it as squarely as can be. I was astounded by how far it went. With what felt like a half swing, the 8-iron flew a lot farther than the 7-irons I was hitting earlier. It only took about 10 balls to engrain that feeling into my memory bank forever. The ease, the power and the purity all put together in one fluid motion. This is too easy, I thought. Too good to be true.

The only other thing we worked on that day was my finish. Instead of dissecting all the intricacies of my swing, he had me make easy half-swings and hold my finish right at the target. If my shoulders were squared up, the ball flew directly at the target with just a tiny bit of draw. If I swung too hard and ended up with my shoulders pointing left, that's where the ball went. If I got lazy and left my shoulders open, the ball went right. Duh. It's not rocket science.

For the first time in my life I wasn't confused after leaving a lesson. Rather than tearing my swing apart piece by piece Andy helped me pull it all together. I didn't get worse before I got better. In fact, I went out the next day and played better than I had in months. The clarity that I experienced on the range with Andy applied immediately to my game. Even my pitch shots and my putts were settling closer to the hole. I don't know what he did, and I don't care. All I know is, it was one of those rare moments in golf when everything just clicked. And now I can go to the driving range or the course and I can recapture that feeling without fail.

THE USUAL APPROACH ISN'T EXACTLY A PICTURE OF EFFICIENCY.

I'm lucky. My experience with Andy changed my whole outlook on the game and inspired this book. Unfortunately, most people will relate more closely with my earlier, less productive lessons. There's an old tee-box joke that says, "if you think you're playing bad now, just try taking a lesson." Sadly, that's how many decent players look at it.

> "I wish there were a Hippocratic Oath for golf teachers because I think most golfers have been harmed by the way golf has been taught over the years."
>
> **– Jim Flick**

A lot of golf instruction just goes in one ear and out the other. Either the student doesn't understand the information that's been presented, or he can't assimilate it. That is, he can't translate the tips into something he can use on the golf course, no matter how many balls he hits. He comes away from the first hour-long session overloaded with detailed explanation of all his faults and burdened with a new "swing" that feels about as natural as a playing left handed. As Leslie Neilson says, most lessons produce an overwhelming feeling of total wrongness.

It's kind of like listening to a management guru giving a motivational speech. You come out of the seminar all pumped up and full of hope. You go back to the office brimming with confidence, thinking you can finally instigate some positive changes and then a week later it's back to the same old frustrations.

Golf instruction hasn't changed much in the last 50 years — not for the average hacker anyway. The vagaries of the English language still sabotage the communication between student and teacher, just as they did in Bobby Jones' day. (There aren't any new words to help describe how a swing should feel, although there are some suggestions for better semantics throughout this book.) Human nature being what it is, ego will always enter into the equation. The title PGA golf "Professional" does not automatically make someone a great golf instructor, any more than the title "Professor" makes someone a great educator.

The relationship between the golf student and the teacher hasn't evolved at all. Most instructors still position themselves as swing doctors — experts at diagnosing your fatal ailments and dispensing over-the-counter medications in the form of a fix... "For the temporary relief of the pain and suffering caused by a faulty golf swing." But that makes you the patient, and we all know how that feels. Instead of being an active participant in the process we become passive recipients of whatever the doctor prescribes. Usually it's a battery of intrusive tests followed by cosmetic surgery. Lobotomies are extra.

Let's face it. Most people aren't getting golf lessons, they're getting swing lessons. And that's the best-case scenario. Worst case, they're getting "hitting" lessons. They aren't learning how to play the game, they're getting a hodgepodge of helpful hints and tips, and 99 out of 100 are focused entirely on the mechanics of hitting the ball.

Despite the bias toward mechanics, golf instruction always has been, and always will be, a very subjective discipline. Doesn't matter how many high tech tools they use, instructors will always resemble economists. None can agree with what's wrong, much less agree on the best course of action. A good case in point comes from a 30-year-old *Golf Magazine* article entitled "If I Had 10 Minutes With Miller." Ten well-know teachers were asked to analyze Johnny Miller's swing. Out of ten instructors, they identified six different "problems" that Miller needed to fix. And not one of them agreed on the best way to do that.

To be honest, teaching is probably a lot harder today than it was 50 years ago. Used to be, only the richest, most well-educated people were ever gullible enough to take up the game. Most of the students had Ivy League educations and were pretty well locked-in to one country club and thus, one teacher.

Today the game is attracting people from all walks of life. People from all demographic and socioeconomic segments are free-lancing around, playing at a different municipal course or up-scale daily-fee course every time out. They're not tied to one particular pro. There is no loyalty. But there is an inexhaustible supply of instructional information out there. Players are bombarded with tips and advice, to the point of paralysis. In fact Andy says the first thing he has to deal with in every lesson is the last thing the pupil read in a magazine. He estimates at least a third of his teaching time is wasted rehashing old baggage and addressing the conflicting opinions that are bandied about as gospel in the magazines and on the golf programs.

Forget about it. If you truly want to learn and improve — if you want to have an epiphany similar to mine — you have to throw out the old paradigm. Forget about how it's always been done, and create a new model for yourself. A model based on having fun every time you're on the course or on the range.

ALL WORK AND NO PLAY MAKES FOR VERY POOR SCORES.

Our culture frowns on people who goof off. From a very early age we're taught to work hard, stay focused, get ahead. All too often play time is construed as counter-productive, even for our children. And once they get out of college, forget about it. Time to buckle to down.

Chuck Hogan says adults don't even know how to play. "The conscious mind, intent on acquiring content, has lost all understanding and appreciation of play." Even when we allow ourselves the time to recreate, we're driven by a work hard/play hard mentality. If we're going to play, we're going do it with some gusto.

That's fine, but it doesn't work very well on the golf course. If you want to perform consistently well, you have to train your conscious mind to get out of the way. Even the pros, who literally go to work on the golf course, say they have to "let it happen." Basically, if you try too hard, and force things to happen, you seldom score very well.

> "Most high achieving adults spend their time primarily in a "training" mind-set. They analyze their performances. They "try" to get better. They "work" at life. They typically need to learn to trust their abilities more. Train and trust are two very different mentalities."
> **-Dr. Bob Rotella**

How many times have you gone out to the golf course "just to screw around" and hit the ball beautifully? How many times have you mentally given up on a round, and then played the last six or seven holes in a zone? Why does that midwinter round, when you haven't touched a club for months, often go so well?

It's because you're not in a working mode, you're in a playing mode. You're engaged in play for play sake, without all the ridiculous expectations that you normally put on yourself. That's the essence of the forget-about-it mindset.

Our goal is to get you into that carefree mindset more often where you can appreciate everything about the game. If you're too careful your mind will be swimming in swing thoughts and you won't be free enough to play up to your potential. If you're careless, you won't have the focus you need to execute the shots and you'll start making sloppy bogies. Carefree is what you want. Your mind is free of mechanical thoughts, you're not worried about outcomes, and you're immersed in the joy of play.

But the carefree, forget-about-it mindset has to start at home and on the practice tee. You can't have an elaborate, mechanical approach to practice and then just change your entire approach the minute you step onto the first tee. As Jim Flick says, "The main reason people tend to work golf instead of play it is that they bring a mechanical approach to the golf course... A mechanical approach to the golf swing is the worst possible way to go when you're trying to *play* golf. "

The first step is to forget about the word "lesson" altogether. Webster's Dictionary defines a lesson as "A section into which a course of study is divided." As in "the manual was broken down into 50 lessons." So by definition, when people take a few golf lessons they're not getting the entire course of study, they're just getting bits and pieces of it. Don't buy into that. Instead of one swing lesson, take the whole course. Or better yet, get some good old-fashioned coaching.

Andy has coached as many as three basketball teams at the same time. A good basketball coach doesn't spend his time giving lessons on the mechanics of shooting free throws. If a player's hitting a bunch of 3-pointers with a slightly unorthodox style, the coach won't jump in and make him change the way he shoots the ball. Forget about it.

Everything a good coach does — everything he says, everything he teaches — is just set-up for game time. He's not trying to develop great technicians. He doesn't care how many 3-pointers his players can hit in practice. His only concern is performance in the game, when it counts. Even the fundamentals are taught in context. Coaches run dozens of drills that instill the fundamentals, while simulating game-time action. They harp on basics in practice, running the three-man weave till their heads spin, so players never have to think about those skills during a game. It's all automatic.

So find a qualified PGA pro who will act as your coach and your mentor. Not your swing surgeon. Loosen up a little and have fun with it. Most instructors make it too much like work. "You gotta work on this or work on that." No you don't. You can choose to work on those specific swing changes by beating balls on the range, but you'd be a lot better off if you had a game to play that addresses the issue in context. Like the three-man weave.

A FEW THINGS YOU SHOULD KNOW
BEFORE YOU FIND A COACH.

Okay. Let's assume for a minute that you've weaned yourself off all the books, magazines and instructional videos. You have the right clubs, customized and fitted to your ability. You've figured out what your learning style is, right brained kinesthetic, left brained visual or whatever. You've even embraced this concept of a new paradigm of learning. Now you only have two things left to do.

First, figure out what type of golfer you are. Do an honest assessment of your skills your scores and your knowledge. Are you a "lost jock," with lots of natural athletic ability but very little understanding of the game. Are you a "rocket scientist" who's spent years studying the swing only to remain at the same-old level. Maybe you're a "naïve beginner" just wanting to experience the game for the first time. Or maybe you're a scratch player who's looking to compete on the next level.

Of the 26.4 million people who play golf, only six percent can break 80 regularly. No one ever "masters" this game, yet we still try. Because for most people, it's not about breaking par, it's about doing your own personal best. It's about holing a long putt or beating your buddy for the first time. It's about the hope that's built into every new club or the opportunities of a short par-5. It's about all the tiny little victories that keep you coming back, even when the wheels fall off.

> "Many teachers ignore feel. They don't trust a student's instincts. They put him in positions and then tell him to move his body and the club until he achieves those positions. The great teachers know that golf is a motion game and that positions are only an early stepping stone to creating the motion."
>
> **– Davis Love Jr.**

Whatever the case, assess your entire game honestly and accurately. Ignoring all mechanical thoughts, write down your strengths and weaknesses. If you don't know, keep some stats for a few rounds and find out how many putts you take, how many balls you lost, how many chips you flubbed. Write down all the negatives, but don't dwell on them. The objective is to find something you can build on, so focus on what you do well.

Your assessment shouldn't be limited to your swing or to your distance off the tee. You also want to consider your motivation and your mental approach to the game. Ask yourself, "why am I doing this? What do I want to get out of this crazy game? How does it make me feel?" (I know, it sounds hokey, but bare with us a minute.) If golfing just leaves you irritated and grumpy all the time, why do it? For some people, it's simply not enough to just go out and enjoy a friendly round of golf. They have to compete. They have to win to get anything out of it. That's a totally different approach than the guy who just wants to hit a few good shots at the annual corporate outing.

For a lot of women, the motivation is simple. They just want to spend time with their husbands during retirement, and the only way to do that is on the golf course. They're realistic. They don't want to be great golfers, but they don't want to embarrass themselves either.

Once you've looked in the mirror and sized up your game it's time to set some goals. Without goals, you can't possibly evaluate the success of your lessons. Not objectively anyway. Goals will help clarify your expectations, which will help your coach tremendously. As Steven Covey says, "We create many negative situations by simply assuming that our expectations are self-evident and that they are clearly understood."A good coach should ask, but if not, you have to communicate those goals clearly.

Given your skills, your time commitment and your mind set, what do you want to accomplish? Make your goals specific, make them realistic and write them in a positive, motivational tone. Don't say "I want to stop three-putting." That's not positive and it's not realistic. Everyone three-putts occasionally, especially if you play a course with big greens. Instead, declare it this way: "I'm going to improve my putting." Then break it down into doable chunks. Maybe you start by improving your short-putt percentage. You can get away with a lot of lousy lag putts if you're deadly from five feet in. Or maybe you need to sharpen your iron or your chipping so you're not left with so many long putts.

Give your goals a time frame. The pros have some built-in deadlines for their personal goals, like qualifying for the Masters or the Tour Championship. You might have a winter goal, and a golf season goal. Or maybe it's a springtime thing where you're getting your game in shape for summer. Whatever your goals are, make them specific and be prepared to share them with your coach. Now you're ready to start the recruiting process.

THE INTERVIEW PROCESS— WHAT TO LOOK FOR IN A COACH.

Teaching pros love working with people who are committed to learning. So when they see that you have good hard questions, and that you're serious about finding an instructor who's a really good fit, they'll probably be enthusiastic about working with you. But don't let their enthusiasm cloud your judgment. Don't be afraid to screen them carefully, as if you're hiring someone for a key position in your company.

It boils down to three things: teaching philosophy, personality and communication skills. You need a coach whose overall philosophy fits your approach to learning. You have to be comfortable with that person. You have to like him well enough to genuinely enjoy your time together. And finally, you need a coach who communicates well with you. If any of these criteria are missing, you'll be back to square one in no time, shopping around for an instructor who you really connect with. So before you make your decision, try to cover these issues and or questions:

> "I never teach by telling what not to do. My job is to teach you what to do. You probably will do plenty of things wrong without any suggestions from me."
>
> **– Tommy Armour**

♦ Avoid the fault & fix mentality. Harvey Penick had great advice for other instructors. He said, "Criticism from a teacher can kill the pupil's ambition to improve. Be anxious to praise and slow on fault-finding." Grill your prospective instructor on this. We all have enough faults to keep an instructor busy for a lifetime, that's not the point. You want someone who will build you up, not tear you down. Someone who's encouraging, not discouraging. There are plenty of positive things an instructor can do with you that will, in turn, fix some of the inconsistencies in your swing. So if he's going to dwell on the negative aspects of your swing, keep calling around.

♦ Find someone who isn't afraid to shut up. Constant yakking is a sure sign of insecurity. You don't want an instructor who force feeds you endless information. A good instructor or coach will spoon feed you tiny little tidbits of information and then wait until you've obviously assimilated the information and applied it before he moves on to something else. It's the only way to combat the confusion problem that overwhelms so many students.

♦ Find someone likable. You don't want Bobby Knight for a

golf coach. You want an encouraging mentor who will gently guide you through the learning process, not someone who's going to fly off the handle the first time you revert back to your old bad habits. If you find someone who seems like a good candidate get some personal references and call them. Better yet, meet him in person. As they say in politics, get some face time with him. That's the best way to make a connection, or not.

◆ Communication skills are the top priority. Believe it or not, the effectiveness of a teacher hinges more on speaking and listening skills than on playing ability. Great instructors listen intently and connect easily with people. They're astute observers of human behavior and they can recognize when a student's eyes are beginning to glaze over. They show and they tell using simple, descriptive language that will clarify, not confuse.

◆ Playing lessons should be part of the package. If you're embracing the concept of play for play's sake, you certainly should get a playing lesson at some point. This is a great way to test his ego. Some teachers don't want to be put in the position of being a caddy for their students. They prefer the superiority of the doctor-patient relationship.

◆ Ask about his mentors. Who does he admire on tour? Whose swing does he pattern his own after? You can learn a lot by simply sitting down in his office and looking at his bookshelf. If he's a Hogan fan he might demand more practice than you're willing to give. If he's interested in golf architecture he might have a more artistic, visual approach to learning. The trick is to find some common ground between you, and then build on it.

◆ Ask about the toughest lesson he's ever given. Find out how he deals with difficult students and how he gauges the success of a lesson. Also ask about the best lessons he's ever given. His memories should be vivid. If he can't remember, he's probably giving a lot of ho-hum lessons that are getting mediocre results.

◆ Ask about video. Many instructors these days depend way too much on video analysis. They record your swing and then spend the next hour comparing all the angles and movements to an "ideal model" like Tiger Woods. Forget about it. For the average golfer this is probably the worst possible method of instruction there is. It does nothing to teach feel. It focuses all your attention on tiny little faults. And it's totally visual. So if your personal learning style is auditory, tactile or kinesthetic, you're in trouble.

Too many players shop for instructors by trial and error. They take a lesson, test the water, and try again. Forget about it. The interviewing process is not foolproof, but it will eliminate 80 percent of the obvious mismatches. It's a process, but it will save you time, money and frustration in the long run.

FORGET ABOUT THE INSTANT CURE. THE GOAL IS LONG-TERM IMPROVEMENT.

Golfers live on instant gratification. The one pure drive that rolls 20 yards past all the other balls. The miraculous 5-iron that settles a few feet from the pin. The scrambling par from way out in the lumberyard. Those moments are what keep people coming back week after week.

Unfortunately, most players also expect that same kind of instant gratification from a lesson. They're looking for that one clear moment when everything comes together, and they're disappointed if they don't achieve it.

Forget about it. If you're looking for an instant cure you're just setting yourself up for failure. What you should be striving for is long-term improvement. It's like the difference between a weekend sales promotion and a long-term marketing strategy. You can get a big boost from the weekend sale, but it's not going to strengthen your brand or increase your market share.

"There are only two things that can keep you from achieving your goals... your willingness to work intelligently and your ability to be patient with regard to your results."
— Dave Pelz

Most golfers who are practicing the binge and purge approach live in a constant state of wonder. As in, "I wonder if I'm going to find my swing today." "I wonder if my putting's going to be off." "I wonder if I'm going to hit that old snap hook today."

If you're in that state of wonder you probably spend countless hours on the driving range in what can only be categorized as a pure experimentation mode. The pattern is pretty predictable. You have a bad round so you go to the range and fish around for something that will help straighten things out. Tapping into your vague recollection of endless tips and articles, you try this and try that until something clicks. And players can pull it off to some degree. That is, you can make some sort of positive correction — enough to make you feel like you've accomplished something.

Well, don't bet on it. Any short-term changes or adjustments you make on the driving range are simply masking the underlying problems and creating a false sense of accomplishment. Until you know what your underlying problems are, there's no way to make any lasting, positive changes.

Just about anyone can find a way to hit the ball decently on the driving range. That's not the point, and that's not how we should measure success. What you're going for is consistency. You need to develop a foundation of repeatable skills you can depend on every time you go out, so you're not fishing around hoping to find your swing or your putting stroke.

Wouldn't it be much simpler — much more efficient — to eliminate the experimentation and the sense of wonder by spending an hour with your coach? With someone who's familiar with your old habits and tendencies. Even if you don't make great strides in your first session, that's okay. Don't worry about it. At least you'll know you're not spinning your wheels. At least you can be confident that you're not making changes just for the sake of change or ingraining new bad habits. Instead, you'll be learning positive new skills and building a foundation for a good, dependable golf game.

The binge and purge approach is a uniquely unproductive method of learning. I know, I was a devout student of that method for years. I could almost always "work through" my problems on the driving range. But in hindsight, I know I wasn't really correcting anything. I was just making short-term changes and compensating for a fundamental problem that I never knew I had.

As it turns out, I was setting up consistently right of the target. From that position I had to get the clubhead pretty well closed on impact if I wanted the ball to go to the target. And there are many, many ways to do that.

You see how it goes? I was never addressing the underlying causes of my problem, but always finding some new band-aid solution. I made all sorts of athletic adjustments to my swing to compensate for this fundamental problem, but it was all just a series of well-executed, short-term corrections for problems that I couldn't even explain. Forget about it. If you want to start improving, you have to quit experimenting.

YOUR FIRST SESSION WITH YOUR NEW COACH — FOCUS ON FUNDAMENTALS.

What do pro baseball players do every spring? They go to spring training and work on fundamentals. Fielding. Batting. Turning the double play. In football, it's basic blocking and tackling. Hit 'em high. Hit 'em low. Pile on.

In golf, it's grip, aim and stance. Before you practice anything else, just put on the gas. Grip. Aim. Stance. Get those three things consistently right and your shot making is going to improve. Guaranteed. It's a simple, positive chain reaction... the correct grip, with the proper aim and a solid stance will produce good results. Even if your swing is quirky or unorthodox, you can still play well.

It's amazing how people can play this game for 10, 20 even 30 years without ever learning these basic building blocks of the swing. It seems like a no-brainer. Every instruction book ever written covers these things. And yet it's the simple little mistakes that continually haunt the average golfer. Grip, aim and stance, in that order.

> "Nine out of ten problems with the swing of the average golfer begin with the grip or the stance. The symptoms that come from these two sources are many and various. It's easy for the teacher to get caught up in treating the symptoms without first going to the underlying causes in the grip and the stance."
> **–Harvey Penick**

On the other hand, many players who have been around the game for some time believe they have the fundamentals down pat and they don't want to "waste" time in a lesson covering stuff they already know. Forget about it. Any problem you have can probably be traced back to the fundamentals.

It's proven that minor changes in the fundamentals can produce major improvement, but those minute changes can also be very disconcerting, especially for tactile and kinesthetic learners.

Grip changes are a good example. Even the slightest change in how you hold the club will feel wrong at first. Not just weird or uncomfortable, but downright wrong. Even though your coach is telling you it's the right thing to do, and you know in your head he's right, it will feel wrong. Your head will tell you one thing and your senses will tell you another.

That's when you need patience, persistence and absolute trust in your coach. For a right-brained tactile learner, this disconnection between what's known and what's felt can be hard to overcome. It will feel like there's absolutely no hope of hitting the ball solidly without doing some drastic manipulations of the club.

In the case of a grip change, left-brained visual learners will have an easier time of it. It'll still feel weird, but they won't be so sensitive to it. Once they get used to the new look of the grip, they'll move on.

The easiest way to learn a new grip is to just hold the club while you're sitting around watching TV or working in your office. Pick it up, take your new grip, and just feel it. Doesn't even have to be a whole club, it could be just the grip end of a club, cut off. Pick it up and set it down. Pick it up and set it down. Do that a few thousand times and your new grip will feel quite natural when you get back out on the driving range.

If you go into the first session with your coach knowing that you'll be working on fundamentals it'll take a lot of pressure off you. The way some players sweat in a lesson you'd think they were on the fist tee at Augusta National with Jack, Arnold and Tiger. Forget about it. Your nerves come from the natural desire to perform well for your new coach, but performing well is not the objective of the session. Learning is. If you want to learn, you gotta forget about it. Remember, you're not there to impress anyone, you're there to learn.

A good way to stave off the butterflies is to arrive 15 minutes early and stretch out. Hit enough balls to find your tempo but not so many that you start thinking about any technical issues. Then, when your coach arrives, spend a few minutes just getting comfortable with him. In order to get the communication process off on the right foot, share your goals, your frustrations and your expectations. Be honest. But try to forget about the mechanical issues that have been clouding your mind. Don't spend your time trying to explain what you think is wrong with your swing. Any decent coach will spot the problem soon enough.

Unfortunately, many people gauge the value of a lesson by the number of balls they hit and the quantity of helpful hints they come away with. Forget about it. Some of the best lessons don't involve hitting balls at all. Instead, simply talking with your new coach is sometimes the best use of time. Or you might be clipping dandelions in your backyard or getting the feel of a new grip in the comfort of your family room.

KEEP IT SIMPLE. MINIMIZE THE CONFUSION.

Here's a fact. It's virtually impossible to prevent confusion from entering into the learning process. You can minimize it by sticking to our information diet, but you'll never eliminate it completely. Even if you find a coach that's a perfect match and you trust that guy with your life, eventually he's going to say something, or show you something, that's just not going to penetrate that thick skull of yours. You just won't get it, no matter how hard you both try.

So the question is, what do you do? How should you and your coach proceed when it seems like the learning has ceased?

First of all, you need to realize that you're the only one who knows what's going on in your head. Your coach can't read your mind, so you need to be aware of your feelings and be assertive enough to say something. If you're feeling confused you have to stop what you're doing and confess that you're in the dark. Just say, "Hey, I'm not tracking with you on that. Is there some other way you can explain that to me?"

If you don't verbalize your confusion — and if your coach doesn't recognize your deer-in-the-headlights look — he might push on and just make things worse. Again, you have to remember it's not a contest. You're not there to perform for your coach, you're there to learn from him. So be honest with yourself and with your coach. He's not there to judge you, he's there to help. So get out of the way and let him do his job.

> "About 90 percent of my pupils arrive for instruction in utter confusion."
> – Tommy Armour

There are all sorts of things that can sabotage a perfectly good session with your coach. Often it's something you recently read or heard that's conflicting with what your instructor is telling you. Forget about it. Magazine articles are written for the masses. The author doesn't know your swing, and your friends who have been giving you all those great tips really want to beat your pants off. So when in doubt, always ignore everything except your coach's instructions.

Sometimes it's the environment... too many people around, too much wind, too cold, or whatever. If you're an audio learner it might just be a couple specific words that are throwing you off or maybe the sound of the hit. Have your coach verbalize it differently.

On the other hand, he might not be saying enough. If you're an audio learner it'll drive you nuts if your instructor just stands back and says nothing. The silence will kill your concentration.

If you're a visual learner you might be having trouble visualizing the new concept. Have the pro show you photos of someone else, or have him demonstrate it himself and watch from several different angles. In this case, a picture's worth a thousand words.

If you're tactile or kinesthtic, you probably aren't getting the "feel" for what your coach is trying to explain. Have him physically walk you through the drill. Let him put you in the right position, then close your eyes and just let your senses absorb the feeling of it. And take your glove off. It's a simple little thing, but for some people it can make a big difference.

Most of the time, confusion stems from trying too much too soon. So rule number one is, don't bite off more than you can chew in the first session. Good coaches know this, and only work on one thing at a time. Experimentation has no place in a golf lesson. If your instructor starts saying things like, "why don't you try this," or, "why don't you try that," stop right there.

Some days you just have too many other things on your mind to absorb anything of any value. In that case, just reschedule the session or change the venue from the practice tee to the green. Go putt for dime skins. If it's really not clicking, there's no use forcing it. You'll just leave more confused and frustrated than when you started.

After you've had a good, productive session it's essential to recap everything before your instructor leaves you to your own devices. Paraphrase what you *think* he wants you to work on. You have to be perfectly clear on this, so repeat what you've taken away from the lesson; show him what you're going to practice and make sure you understand it. Then write it down, verbatim. (Some instructors will do that for you.) Remember the exact words your coach used — the verbiage is very important. If he said "swing the clubhead" don't write down "swing the club." They're two different things. If he said "make a full shoulder turn,"don't write down "make a full turn."

If you have any questions or nagging concerns, get the answers before you start practicing on your own. The last thing you want to do is spend the next two weeks on the practice range instilling a bad habit.

For visually oriented people it may also help to get some photos from your instructor that help illustrate the ideas you've been working on. This is one time when magazines can come in handy. For instance, Andy often works with people on the finish position because it's a good indicator of what's happened with the rest of the swing. Looking at a still photo of Tom Watson's square, well-balanced finish can be inspiring.

Video is another popular tool that many instructors use. Unfortunately, it seems to cause as much confusion as clarification. Most students simply don't know what they're looking at. They see all sorts of differences when their swing is compared to some perfect pro, but they can't really see what the instructor is talking about. The subtleties are lost on them.

The whole idea of video analysis is contrary to the forget-about-it approach. Stop-motion video allows you to break down the swing piece by piece in excruciating detail, and the minute you start down that path you're in for trouble. It's a classic symptom of the binge and purge approach to learning. You try some new technique for awhile and then look at your swing on video. If it doesn't look better you go back and try something else. It's an endless cycle.

However, the video camera can be a useful feedback tool if the student doesn't believe what his instructor is telling him. It's that perception problem we talked about. A video camera can set you straight real quick and provide definitive proof that what you think you're doing is not really what you're doing. In this case, it's more for the instructor than for the student.

So if you want to get the most out of your lessons and avoid confusion, stay away from video. It will just encourage more nit-picking of your swing. Instead, listen to your instructor, he's the best source of feedback you can get.

Another source of high priced confusion is golf school. You can easily drop a couple grand to spend a week completely immersed in every nuance of the game. Your swing will be dissected every which way, you'll learn dozens of drills and you'll come away filled with hints, tips and thoroughly helpful advice from pros you'll never see again.

Forget about it. For 99 percent of you it's just too much information all at one time. It's like reading a half dozen different instruction books in one week. You'll be imparted with great knowledge, but you never have a chance to apply anything long enough to ingrain it into your subconscious. Just when you think you're starting to get it, you're moving on to the next segment of the program. And it's not an individualized deal. You have to stick with curriculum that's designed to appeal to a wide audience, even if it means spending a full day on the one part of your game that you're perfectly comfortable with.

We're not saying that all golf schools are a complete waste of time. It's just that most will inundate you with enough technical information to last a lifetime and it's very difficult to translate all that into usable skills. If you could have follow-up lessons with one of the school's instructors every two weeks for a year, you might begin to make sense of it.

Some schools limit their instruction to one specific part of the game. Short game schools, for instance, can be helpful as long as they don't get too technical. But even then, you'll walk away feeling overwhelmed. The cardinal rule about not practicing more than one or two new things at a time goes right out the window.

So forget about the crash-course. A simpler, more productive approach is to find an instructor you really like and then put together a long-term learning program that leaves plenty of time for practice between sessions. That way you can get more than just information. You also get the coaching and the encouragement you need to make continuous improvements in your game.

LEARNING INVOLVES CHANGE, SO GET USED TO IT.

Some people have a real hard time with change. Doesn't matter if it's a career change or a simple change in the golf swing, some people really fear it. They operate in a very small comfort zone, and anything outside of that is met with great resistance.

On the other hand, there are some people who thrive on change. They accept every one of life's changes as a golden opportunity for something new and great to happen. They aren't stuck in their ways. They're open to suggestion as long as it moves them closer to their goal. And they're adaptable. For golf instructors, this is a much easier crowd to work with.

If you want to get the most out of your golf lessons it helps to have a little bit of that adaptability. Even if it's completely against your nature, at some point you're going to have to suck it up and embrace the discomfort.

> "Any change that's dictated is change resisted."
> **–Dr. Spence Johnson,**
> From *Who Moved My Cheese*

The most common source of discomfort is the grip. Nobody walks up to a golf club for the very first time and grips it in the PGA-prescribed manner. It's just not natural. Unfortunately the natural grip doesn't work very well. (Technicians would say it doesn't deliver the clubhead squarely to the ball on a consistent basis.) Therefore, just about every one of you is going to have to change your grip at some time or another, and when you do, it's going to feel really, really weird. Your brain will be telling you it's wrong, your body will compensate with all sorts of odd swings and your tendency will be to revert back to the comfort of your old grip.

When you're trying to master a major change like that it takes every ounce of patience to stick with it. What you want to do is forget about results for awhile and just focus only on the sensation of the proper grip. If you get hung up on results and start reacting to where each shot goes, you'll just compensate for the new grip with some sort of hackneyed swing change. Pretty soon you're not only doubting the new grip, but you're doubting your entire swing. That's what a lot of people experience when they get the sinking feeling that they're getting a lot worse before they get better.

Forget about it. You can't work on a new swing and a new grip at the same time. And you can't expect immediate results. As we said in Chapter 2, it's a process, not a panacea.

In the case of golf instruction, the fear of change is often rooted in doubt. Doubt that you can do what your instructor would like you to do. Doubt that the change will stick. And even doubt that he's giving you good advice. That's another reason to find an instructor with a similar mindset who you really trust. You have to forget about it. Good instructors will never have you make changes just for the sake of change or merely to justify their fee. There's always a goal in mind — an outcome that will result in better play. You might not understand how the changes are going to work, but that's okay. That's why you hire a coach.

Maybe we should all just forget about the word change altogether. The word change connotes throwing something out and starting over, but in golf you're always building on the skills you already have. Perhaps it'd be better to think in terms of adjustments. You're making a minor adjustment in your grip or you're fine-tuning your putting stroke.

Whatever you want to call it, change is inevitable. Your game will either change for the worse, or change for the better. It's up to you to decide.

4
THE FORGET-ABOUT-IT GUIDE TO PRACTICE

"Discipline yourself to take your time and practice one shot at a time. Don't rush through the shots, but instead practice with a purpose. In essence, learn to practice how you play. I think you'll be surprised by the results."

—WALLY ARMSTRONG

You know the old cliché, "practice makes perfect?" Well forget about it. As Bob Rotella says, golf is not a game of perfect. Even if you practiced 40 hours a week you'd never master all the subtleties of the game. There's always something to improve upon, even if you're Tiger Woods.

Instead of perfect, try the word permanent. "Practice makes permanent." If you practice well and practice often, you can add shots to your permanent repertoire that you never dreamed of pulling off. With good coaching and focused practice you can learn to hit a low hook when you really need to, even if a high fade is the mainstay of your game. You can learn to use that lob wedge that you've been carrying around for three years. You can chip with your 3-wood or play the Texas wedge with the best of them. But only if you practice with purpose.

Most players, if they practice at all, do it randomly. Just stop and watch the typical line-up at the driving range. Nine out of 10 people are swinging for the bleachers with the biggest club in the bag. Once they've parked a few good ones they move on down through the bag, blasting 3-woods, 5-woods and maybe a few 7-woods until all the balls are gone. It's a robotic, rapid fire exercise in futility for the most part.

If you want to learn to play the game with any degree of proficiency, you're going to have to learn to practice all the skills you need on the course. That doesn't mean putting in long hours at the driving range, it means playing real golf shots to an intended target every time. It means going through the pre-shot routine and getting good, accurate feedback on your misses. It means hitting wedge shots from the rough, and yes, it even means spending time on and around the practice green.

For many people it's just too much to ask. They simply don't have the time to waste their precious days off chipping and putting. Others don't have the patience for it. They want results, and they want them now. And then there are the players who are just plain happy with how they play. Doesn't matter that they seldom break 90 or 100, they're content with their mediocrity. In a way, I envy those guys. They have an admirable "forget about it" mindset, but they also have very little chance of ever improving.

Before you start a good practice routine you should decide which group you fit into. If you're like me — an over-informed under-achiever who really wants to get better — then by all means, get with a good coach and start practicing. But if you just want to go out and slap it around a few times a summer, then forget about it. Don't waste your time whacking balls. Just hit a few as a warm-up before each round and spend enough time on the practice green to get a feel for the greens. Then play your game and be happy with whatever happens.

If you're taking the time to read this book, chances are you don't fit into that care less category. You do want to play better, and you will need to practice. So get a good coach and get going.

PRACTICE BRIDGES THE GAP BETWEEN KNOWLEDGE, LEARNING AND PERFORMANCE.

Do you know how many people there are who have acquired a wealth of knowledge about the golf swing without ever developing the skills they need to play the game? They're out there, believe me. They talk big, like they know it all, and then spray shots all over the course and can't break 90. Without adequate practice, all you have is knowledge for knowledge sake.

On the other hand, there are many perennial contenders who know very little about the golf swing. You've probably been beaten by one of these guys. They often have unorthodox swings, but they get up and down a lot. They keep the ball in the fairway, they make very few mental blunders, and they manage to win club events on a regular basis.

In which group would you rather belong?

The men and women who win on a regular basis, at any level, know how to practice without over-analyzing things. They probably have a reasonable amount of knowledge about the fundamentals but they don't concern themselves with too many details. Somehow they're able to just forget about it and focus on the skills they need to get the ball in the hole.

> "Once you have learned the art of swinging, the degree of skill you develop will be the result of your intelligent application of that knowledge through practice. Habit, subconsciously controlled, is the result only of frequent repetition."
> **- Ernest Jones**

That's what it's all about. Skill, not knowledge. If you want to perform well on the course you'll need analytical skills to assess each shot and make sound decisions. You need creative skills to visualize the shot. And finally, you need physical skills and coordination to swing the club. If you want to improve, you have to hone all these skills, not just the physical act of hitting a ball.

Skill building begins by absorbing some basic information. For instance, if you want to practice a high, soft-landing pitch shot, you need to know what club to use, how to set up for the shot, and how to get the high trajectory. (The best way to gather that information is through a hands-on demonstration with your coach, not from a book or a magazine.)

But knowing how to hit the shot is a far cry from having the skill to do it consistently. Somehow you have to translate your knowledge into a physical sensation. You have to develop the "feel" of hitting the shot by doing it over and over again with positive results.

Finally, the most important step is to ingrain that positive feeling to the point that it becomes habit. You simply have to practice it over and over again until you completely trust your ability to execute the shot. Learning to trust your training is probably the hardest part of the entire process.

A lot of people talk about muscle memory, but your muscles don't remember things, your mind does. It's your brain that instructs the muscles to perform in a certain way. If you make a terrible golf swing it's not your muscles that are failing you, it's your brain that's gone haywire. For whatever reason, your muscles aren't getting the right signals from your brain.

In order for something like a golf shot to become habit, you have to practice it until you can forget about it. Isn't that the definition of instinct? Routine and repetition enable to you play a shot instinctively once you've practiced it enough. As Chuck Hogan says, it must be "imprinted without ambiguity" in your mind, and you can only accomplish that through repetition and practice.

So you see, the learning process is entirely dependant on practice. Without practice, your knowledge won't amount to a hill of beans. Conversely, without some knowledge, your practice won't be the least bit constructive. So if you want to shorten the learning curve, get with a good coach, and put the two together.

FORGET ABOUT YOUR BIGGEST SWING AND PRACTICE THE LITTLE STUFF.

Jack Nicklaus said, "setup is the single most important maneuver in golf." Dr. Bob Rotella, one of the preeminent sports psychologists in the game, calls the preshot routine the rod and the staff of the golfer under pressure. The foundation of consistency. Jim Flick says that set-up accounts for 80 percent of the swing's effectiveness — or ineffectiveness. That means eight out of 10 of your bad golf shots are missed before you ever swing the club! Either your aim was off, you made the wrong decision, you weren't fully committed, didn't visualize it, or whatever. There are a hundred little things that can go wrong before you ever take the club back.

That's why it's so important to practice in a patient, disciplined manner, rather than just hitting balls. The idea is to treat each ball as if it's the most important shot of a really good round of golf. You practice the entire process of playing the shot, from initial preparation through shot evaluation. You don't just work on your swing, you practice incorporating all the little things that go into a good golf shot so when you get to the course you can forget about it and just play.

Bob Toski and Jim Flick recognized the importance of the setup long ago. In *How To Become A Complete Golfer* they said that amateurs come to them for help on the swing, while touring pros want help on their setup — posture, aim and body alignment. "The pros realize one of the most-ignored principles in golf: your setup dictates the way you swing a golf club, and your swing can only be as consistent as that setup."

So forget all the mechanical thoughts and practice getting the basic set-up consistently right. Even though it may seem elementary, the best players constantly check their grip, aim and stance — the fundamentals of a good setup. They practice getting the ball positioned correctly for each particular shot, be it a driver or a short iron approach. They practice different set-ups for hitting into the wind or compensating for a crosswind. They develop the habit of aiming at an intermediate target just a few yards in front of them. They constantly check their alignment. Instead of just whacking balls, they use disciplined repetition to ingrain good habits that they can take to the course.

> **"Your practice habits carry over to the golf course, so if you want to have the best possible playing habits, you had better develop them on the practice tee. If you are to be a good player, you will never stop working on your setup."**
> **— Jim Flick**

Compared to the complex set of motions in a golf swing, the setup is a mindlessly simple thing to get right. But a good setup isn't just going to come to you. You have to train yourself to get the grip, the aim and the stance right every time.

The fact is, eight in 10 golfers consistently line up too far to the right. They might get their bodies pointing at the target, but not the clubface. I know it's one of my oldest bad habits, and it has caused all sorts of problems in my swing. Yet nobody practices aiming the clubhead and then aligning their feet parallel to the target. Nobody seems to bother with good posture. Nobody, except for the most successful pros, practice with the disciplined repetition they need to develop a dependable routine that they can forget about when they're on the course.

If you want your practice to translate to better play, approach each shot as you would on the course. Especially when you're practicing putting. Use the same type of ball you normally play with. Walk around and scope out the line and the speed of each putt. Do all the little things you normally do on the course, like lining up the logo of your ball with the target. Forget the old three-ball approach to putting practice and start working on your entire putting routine. One ball at a time. (There's more on putting routine in Chapter 6.)

THE BEAUTY OF BEING A BEGINNER.

You may have heard the tale about a about a guy who takes up golf for the simple pleasure of it. He knows nothing about the game; He's had no lessons. He doesn't watch the TV telecasts and he's never laid eyes on a golf magazine. He's a golf virgin.

For a year or so he plays nine holes everyday all by himself. Eventually, he decides he's ready to try a full round, so he accepts an invitation to play with a few friends. They all shoot in the 80's and 90's, while this newcomer posts a two-over 74. Up to that point, this guy thought 72 was an *average* score and was a little disappointed with two over par score. He had no idea how good he really was.

Naturally, all his friends were amazed, and started talking to him about going pro. They figured that if he could shoot even par in less than a year, then he could really go places if he just took a few lessons and worked on his game a little.

"Golf is really a simple game. We make it complex and confusing by our approach to it."

-Greg Norman

Unfortunately, he listened to them. Once he started working on his swing and learning the intricacies of the game, his scores started to soar. The innocence was gone. And he never really enjoyed the game again.

I'm not sure if this tale is true, or if it's just golf folklore handed down from one foursome to the next. But we've all known relative beginners who have gone out and torn up the course. And even a first-timer can hit an occasional shot spectacularly. That's what makes this game so enticing.

If you're new to the game, count your blessings. You have a clean slate. You don't have to spend countless hours replacing old, bad habits with new, good habits and you don't have any expectations weighing you down. So go with it. Have fun just swinging the club, playing the game.

If you're intent on learning the game, you can use your ignorance to your advantage. Assuming you find a competent instructor, you can simplify the learning process dramatically just by ignoring all the advice from your friends and family. Instead, start with the fundamentals and work up from there.

When Andy teaches beginners, he likes to start with the shortest shots, and then work up to the full swing. Like Harvey Penick did. So the first thing his students practice is putting, then they move on to chipping, pitching and finally to the full swing. With each step the swing gets bigger, but the underlying theory stays the same. This progressive, cumulative approach to learning is much more efficient than the trial and error approach. And exactly the opposite of how most people take up the game today.

The usual approach is to hit the driving range a couple times then head out to the course. But the last place you want to try to learn is on the golf course. It's way too intimidating to be a good learning environment. Unless you go out when there's absolutely no one around, there's so much pressure to keep pace and to look good, you might not ever get comfortable.

You don't need a golf course, or even a driving range, to imprint the fundamentals in your mind. You can practice the most basic fundamental of all — the grip — just about anywhere. The idea is to get used to holding a club properly. Do it at home, in your office, wherever. Just hold a club in your hands as your coach taught you. Grip and regrip the club more times than Sergio Garcia under pressure. Keep doing it until it's second nature to you — until you can call it up without the slightest hesitation. Then move on to other, more complicated skills. If you start this way you can forget about making major changes in your grip later on, when it's much more difficult to do.

To avoid confusion, never tackle more than one thing at a time. Don't change your finish position while simultaneously tweaking your takeaway. You won't get anywhere.

If you have to work on a swing change forget about where the ball's going for a while and focus only on the new sensations of the swing. If you focus on the results of each shot you'll be so busy trying to adjust things you'll never ingrain the proper feel. In *The Inner Game Of Golf* Tim Gallwey calls this "awareness instruction." Forget about everything else and devote all your attention to the awareness of how the swing feels.

If you're working on a fundamental skill like a new grip, forget about your swing for the time being. Until your grip is comfortably dialed in there's no way you'll be able to focus your attention on anything else. It's just too uncomfortable. Besides, you may not even need to change your swing once you get the grip right.

A good golf pro will know what your new grip is going to do to the flight of the ball. He'll know how your posture effects your golf swing. He'll understand the cause and effect of such things and will recognize the sequence of changes that need to be made. Or more importantly, not made.

By working with a good coach you won't waste time fiddling with the mechanics of your golf swing when all you really needed was a minor adjustment in your setup or grip. Under the watchful eye of a pro you'll know, for sure, when you're practicing new shots correctly — that is, with proper fundamentals — and not just ingraining bad habits. You won't be led astray by the hair-brained tips offered by well-meaning friends and family members. And you won't waste your time hitting balls from here to kingdom come with no concern at all for the target.

Beginners also have the advantage of rapid, tangible improvement. When you're first starting out you can make big strides in a relatively short amount of time. But the better you get, the harder it gets to make substantial improvement. At some point you'll hit a plateau where you'll be tempted to heave your clubs into the nearest river. Forget about it. As long as you have a foundation of solid fundamentals, and as long as you keep your practice sessions fun, you can always work on some part of your game that will produce positive results.

Dr. Bob Rotella sums it up: "I'm not a great believer in hitting bucket after bucket with the full swing. It's an easy way to develop bad habits. You would be far better off hitting a couple dozen balls three times a week, going through the routine on every ball, picking out a target, and trusting. You'd at least be on your way to ingraining mental discipline and getting the best score out of the swing you have."

Andy has a way of training his students to take more time on every practice shot. If he sees someone hitting a large bucket he simply replaces it with a small one and instructs them to spend just as much time on the range as they would have with the bigger bucket. Same time commitment, half the balls. Try it.

ALWAYS KEEP YOUR EYE ON THE TARGET.

Here's an analogy that might help put your current practice habits into perspective. Imagine you're an accomplished archer. You're thoroughly immersed in the artistry and history of the bow and arrow, and you're practicing for an upcoming competition. But instead of shooting at a traditional target, you go out into a big field and just start launching arrows into the air to see how far they fly.

That's pretty much what goes on at the driving range.

With a "fairway" that's 100 yards wide and no out-of-bounds, it's only natural to swing for the fences. The problem is, after a while, people get so ball bound they forget what the object of the game is. Hitting the ball with the clubhead is *not* it. The object is to get the ball to the target, i.e. in the hole. So the focus of your practice sessions should always be to hit the target, whatever that may be. It's a specific distance and specific direction that you're after, because one without the other won't get you very far.

> "It's important to be target-oriented on each shot... you cannot be position-oriented or swing-oriented while you are playing the game."
> **–Bob Toski**

At the typical, flat driving range the playing field is so broad and undefined it's tough to find a good target. Random flagsticks are not the same as real greens which are almost always surrounded by bunkers and framed by trees, so you have to focus even harder than normal on your chosen target.

The fact is, most players have a very poor sense of where the real target is. They act like the ball is the target, but it's not. The target is way out there, somewhere, out of your field of vision. So before you swing you need to be lined up properly with the target, and when you swing you need to have a clear vision of that target in your mind.

I love it when driving ranges have something tangible and fun to aim at. My neighborhood course always has two oil drums setup less than 80 yards out. Hit it in the barrel and they give you a prize like a burger or a free bucket of balls. The kids love it, and it's great training for my wedge game. My goal is to hit one high floater and one low spinner into the same barrel.

Andy sees people all the time who have no idea where they're going, much less aiming. He'll watch them hit a few balls and then politely ask, "what are you aiming at?" Usually the response is something like "Uhhh, nothing in particular, just right out there somewhere." Okay. So Andy lets him hit a few more and sure enough, they go "somewhere right out there."

If you're not confirming your aim and alignment during your practice sessions you're just wasting your time. When you get on a golf course that's lined with trees or littered with bunkers, you won't have a chance.

In my first lesson with Andy he proved — much to my dismay — that I have a bad habit of lining up inadvertently to the right. Even when I'm acutely aware of what I'm doing, I sometimes line up that way. But over the years I have learned to compensate for that error by shutting the clubface, which in turn causes a number of other problems. The point is, I practiced so much with poor alignment that I eventually created a swing that would get the ball to the target even though I wasn't really aimed at it.

Forget about it. It's a lot easier to aim properly than it is to compensate for lousy aim. Now, every time I practice I lay some clubs down as guides and I make absolutely sure that my alignment and ball position is correct before I ever swing the club. Of course, it seems like I'm aiming left of the target, but that's just my perception. My vision deceives me. I have to learn to trust my guides and retrain my eyes, and I can only get there by practicing diligently with aiming aids and by having dependable feedback. It's the only way to stay target oriented in all my practice sessions.

THE PITFALLS AND PAYOFFS OF EXPERIMENTATION.

The binge and purge approach to learning golf involves constant experimentation. You read about a new technique and you go to the range to try it on for size. If it seems to work, you hang onto it until something new comes along. If it doesn't work, you have to purge the idea from your mind and move on to some other "sure thing."

But without any guidance this experimental approach causes nothing but confusion. And, contrary to what some teachers will tell you, confusion does not lead to enlightenment. It just leads to more confusion. After a few years of this you won't know where you started or where you left off. It's like a sophomore chemistry class where the kids are just throwing stuff together to see what happens. Danger, danger! As Percy Boomer once said, "The self-taught golfer is usually a badly taught one."

The fact is, if most of your practice sessions are spent experimenting with your swing, you're probably doing yourself more harm than good. I spent years experimenting with different putting methods. But with each new method came dozens of new questions. And tons of doubt. Just the act of trying something new has a way of messing with your head because you never completely forget what you were trying two weeks ago or last year. Even though you've moved on to a new and improved method, all that old information is still lodged in your brain somewhere. It didn't go away, and it often comes back to haunt you at the worst possible times.

> "An abundance of what is written on the golf swing is controversial and contradicts other expert views. Point by point. Mixing ideas from totally different concepts can be frustrating and is usually counter-productive."
>
> **– Jim McLean**

There is, however, a positive side to experimentation. Experimentation during practice sessions can lead to improved awareness, and awareness is the gateway to true learning.

In golf, "awareness" and "feel" are almost synonymous. If your goal is to improve your awareness of what the clubhead is doing, you will improve your feel in the process. That's a given. So the idea is to find some exercises that will improve your awareness of key parts of your game.

For instance, if you tend to get too quick and choppy with your swing, you might want to improve your awareness of your tempo. That doesn't mean "working on better tempo," it just means focusing all your attention on the tempo that you have. Once you get out of the mode that says, "I need to fix my tempo" and just open yourself up to better awareness, the results will come automatically.

This is one of the basic tenants of Tim Gallwey's "Inner Game" theory. He says everyone has the natural ability to swing smoothly, you just have to develop awareness of your existing tempo, and then trust yourself enough to swing how you'd like to swing. Like Ernie Els, for instance.

Most people don't have the awareness to know when they've rushed their swing or their routine. They're usually too wrapped up in where the ball's going — or not going — to notice any of the sensations that come with a quickened swing.

So here's the deal. If you want to improve your awareness, you need to forget about the results, suspend judgment and just focus on feelings. (This can be quite a stretch for most men.)

When you're practicing, shift your attention inward and absorb as many details as you can. How does it feel when your swing gets "too quick?" What parts of your body instigate this feeling of quickness? Does your finish feel different when the swing is quicker than normal? What are your hands doing during this quick, jerky swing? Does your head feel like it's bobbing up and down?

Forget about "fixing" these things. And forget about what you're *not* doing. The only goal is to develop objective awareness of what you *are* doing. As Tim Gallwey says, "When a golfer sees his swing in terms of "good" or "bad" he will not have a clear picture of it as it is. Awareness never judges."

So if you're going to experiment with things, do it without judging the results of each shot. Just try something, and focus on how it feels, not on how it works. Ultimately, your improved awareness will help your subconscious, right-brained self hit the ball more smoothly and accurately, without any "work" on your swing.

Another key to productive experimentation is to differentiate between experimenting with your swing, or swing mechanics, and experimenting with actual shots. If you have a good instructor you can learn a lot by experimenting with different shots. You can feel what it's like to intentionally hook the ball. You can see what happens when you move the ball back in your stance or when you open the clubface on a pitch shot.

Experimenting in this way produces good information, but you have to know what to do with it. Otherwise, it's just more stuff cluttering your mind. And don't expect much when you're experimenting. You're not trying for results, you're trying to increase your awareness of what the ball will do in certain situations.

The reason why many players spend so much time experimenting is that they have incomplete or inaccurate feedback on what they're really doing. They think the clubface is open. They read an article on proper torso rotation and decide they must be sliding their hips. They think a lot of things, but they don't know for sure because the feedback isn't reliable.

There are only a few ways to get accurate feedback about what's really going on in your swing: (1) Feel it with your hands. (2) Hear it from an instructor. (3) See it, in a mirror or on video. The problem is, the sensations you get through your hands can be deceiving. And for videotape, you often won't understand what it is you're seeing, especially without an instructor to interpret it for you.

An expert's eye is the most reliable form of feedback there is. Even though two instructors might see things differently, it's better than relying on your own perception or that of a well-meaning friend. A good instructor will help you sift through all the various types of feedback and focus on the information that really matters. (Believe me, there's a lot of stuff about the golf swing that you really don't want to know.) If you've been reading too many articles, he can help translate the terminology for you and tell you what to forget about it. If you're confused by a long pattern of experimentation, he can help make sense of it and get you back to basics. And the longer you work together, the better his feedback becomes.

Percy Boomer once said that most of your trouble is getting rid of false ideas. Some people tell you to swing like Ben Hogan. Others say swing with the tempo of Sam Snead or Ernie Els. Swing hard, like Nick Price. Take the hands out of it, like Tiger Woods. Right, right, right, right. It's all good advice for someone, and if you don't have a pro who knows your game, you won't know what applies and what doesn't.

Another source of great inspiration for experimentation is television. After watching Tiger thoroughly wax the field in yet another major championship, it's tempting to try some of his techniques on the driving range. But Sam Snead was right when he said no swing can be Xeroxed. Everyone has a different swing. Everyone has different things they need to do to improve. Everyone processes information differently. Therefore, what you need is individualized instruction. Not universal tips that go out to a half million subscribers or TV viewers.

If you want to experiment with something, talk to your instructor first. Make sure that it's something worth working on, that it's not going to just cause confusion and contradict the other things you've been working on. Better yet, just stick to the program that your pro prescribed for you to start with.

And whatever you do, don't start experimenting with anything in the middle of a round. In-round experimentation is even worse than experimenting on the practice tee. How many times have you heard frustrated golfers exclaim, "What am I doing?", or "I don't know what I'm doing." They're befuddled because they lack the awareness they need to recognize their most common habits. They see the poor results, but don't know the cause, so they feel helpless to do anything about it. This usually leads to a self-defeating pattern of in-round experimentation… "well, that didn't work, so maybe I'll try this on the next tee." It's pure guesswork and it seldom ever helps a player salvage a good round.

PRACTICE DOESN'T HAVE TO BE WORK.

Ben Hogan was famous for his work ethic. As the story goes, he'd hit balls till his hands bled, saying that the secret of golf lies buried in the turf.

Forget about it. You're not Ben Hogan, and beating balls until your hands bleed is not the solution. There has to be a happy medium—something between Hogan's approach and the non-existent practice routine of the typical weekend hacker.

If you're committed to practicing, but you're not as diligent or methodical as Hogan, you might try putting a little play into your practice. Rather than treating each practice session as a chore, try taking a more playful approach. Embrace your inner child and be creative for a change.

> "A lot of people practice as if they're preparing for the next Showdown at Sherwood. They're just grinding away, getting nowhere fast. Instead, play during practice so you practice how to play "
> **- Andy Heinly**

What? You're not very creative, you say. Or maybe all your creativity has been sucked out of you by too many years in corporate life. Well forget about it. Everyone's creative in some way, that's what makes us human. So use a little creativity when it comes time to practice. Don't just stand there hitting ball after ball to the same spot. Mix it up a little. Play games with yourself.

When you're on the driving range, imagine that you're playing a round at your favorite course. If the first tee requires a bit of a draw, then try to play the draw. If you block the shot out to the right, play the next ball as a recovery shot. Play a low punch, as if you're stymied under some branches, or a high one over the imaginary trees. You can even keep score this way. The point is to make up games that require you to use all your shot making skills, not just the physical ones.

An easy way to turn a ho-hum practice session into a fun, productive day is to get a friend to compete against, or even a foursome. If you're working on your short game pick shots that require a little imagination. Play over your golf bag or under a bench. Call your shot and keep score. Incorporate some chipping and pitching and play the ball all the way into the hole.

No matter what you're working on, it's wise to put some pressure on yourself by putting up a couple bucks. Play for dime skins or a hundred bucks a shot, whichever works for you. Then focus on going through your routine on every single shot. No exceptions. That's the kind of rehearsal that will really pay off when you get on the course. You might even win a few quarters in the process.

Ernie Els developed his languid tempo by hitting a whiffle ball in his backyard. He found that swinging hard at such a ball didn't help a bit. He could swing slow and easy and still get just as much distance. Thus his nickname, "The Big Easy."

Some of the best putters in the world play putt-putt golf. Johnny Miller taught his kids by letting them hit balls into the lake. Harvey Penick had students swinging at dandelions, clipping off the tops. With a little imagination, the possibilities are endless.

The point is, there are plenty of ways to keep things interesting when you practice. It doesn't have to be boring, and it should never resemble work.

Dr. Bob Rotella talks about the training mentality versus the trusting mentality and asserts that you have to spend at least 60 percent of your practice time in the trusting mentality. "In the training mentality a golfer evaluates his shots critically and analytically. In the trusting mentality he simply accepts them. In training, you try to make things happen. In the trusting mentality, you let things happen."

Most people spend all their practice time, and a lot of their playing time for that matter, in the training mentality. They're trying to train their body to do something that will hopefully result in a better golf swing. But if you're going to practice as you play, you need to get out of the training mode and into the trusting mode. That means shutting out all thoughts of technique and mechanics and focusing only on the target and the routine. Turning off that side of your brain is a learned skill. It takes practice, patience and a good bit of determination to accomplish on a regular basis. But without that skill, you can forget about accomplishing your goals in this game.

In the next chapter we talk a lot more about that mental battle that goes on during a round. But for now, remember that if you want your practice to translate into better scores, you can't just hit balls, you have to play real shots. You can't rely on your own gut instinct and a few helpful hints from late night TV. You need guidance and dependable feedback. And you need to practice getting your mind off mechanics.

5
THE FORGET-ABOUT-IT GUIDE TO PLAYING

"The reason people don't shoot low scores, to be blunt, is that most people don't know how to PLAY. Not how to swing, or how to hit the ball farther, how to play the game."

—RAMOND FLOYD

Up to this point, *The Forget-About-It Guide* has been focused primarily on learning the game and putting the pieces in place in order to improve. Now we're getting to the good part. The part where Andy and I reveal our revolutionary new method that's guaranteed to have you shooting in the low 70's!

Okay, maybe not. The truth is, there is no magic formula. No holy grail of golf. Every instructor has a different approach, every method has some potential, and every book holds certain truths. But if you study the game's best players and analyze golf instruction down through history, you'll find three keys that appear over and over again. These aren't tips, they're universal truths that will improve your game. They are: (1) Quit trying so hard and have fun out there. (2) Minimize your mistakes by winning the head game. (3) Sharpen your short game.

If you can do all three of them in one round, you'll be thrilled with your performance. Even if you can nail two out of three a good percentage of the time you'll be ahead of the game. But if you don't do any of the three occasionally, forget about it. Might as well hang up your clubs and join a bowling league.

QUIT TRYING SO HARD AND HAVE A LITTLE FUN WITH IT.

How many people play golf regularly without keeping score? Without attaching a number to their performance? Unfortunately, not too many. A lot of people play tennis just for the exercise, and maybe the satisfaction of hitting the ball back and forth consistently, but in golf it hardly ever happens.

On the golf course it's hard to put the score out of your mind, even if you want to. Even if you just go out with your family and never touch a scorecard, chances are you still have a fairly good idea of how you scored. (You sure as heck keep track when you make a birdie, and you probably know exactly which holes caused major problems.) In the end, you probably have a good feeling for whether you're playing above or below your handicap.

That's because golfers are obsessed with numbers. Everyone talks about the beautiful scenery, but what they're really interested in is the precise yardage, slope and rating. Courses are judged not on aesthetic terms, but by how long they are, and everyone wants to bomb their drives 15 yards farther than the next guy.

> **"Success comes easier when we make an effort, but don't try. The less a golfer tries, the more fluid his swing will be."**
> **– Timothy Gallwey**

And then there's the handicapping system. Before you can even start a round everyone wants to know your number so they can stick a label on you and judge your performance as the game progresses. Might as well give everyone a big name tag to wear around the course: "Hi I'm Bob, I'm a 14 handicap." And the comparisons don't stop there. Armchair players even use numbers to compare themselves to the pros: "Did you see Tiger hit that 4-iron 256 yards over the water?" or "That was a 210 yard 7-iron!"

Numbers can help you get your head around the monstrous complexities of the game. So it's only natural to sum-up your day on the golf course with a nice round number that you can immediately post on an official USGA computer terminal.

The irony of it is, if you want to shoot a low score — and perform up to your potential — you have to forget about scoring. If you're trying to score well it will seldom happen. In fact, the harder you try the bigger the number gets. As Yoda once said, "Try not. Do or do not. There is no try."

Sam Snead said his best results have come when he's hardly trying at all. Once again, we run into a language problem. The word "trying" implies some sort of trouble, as in "It was a trying day on the course." It also suggests that you didn't "do" what you were supposed to do. You only tried. There's also a stigma attached to people who don't "try." If at first you don't succeed, try, try again.

"Making your best effort" is a much better term than "trying." It's more positive. Even if the shot didn't turn out as you planned it was your best effort. Making your best effort has a tone of objectivity that allows you to separate yourself from your shot. "I made my best effort and it still didn't go in. So be it." And finally, it implies some accomplishment. You did it. You gave it your best effort. Horray!

Ask a random sample of people on the driving range what they're trying to do and you'll hear a hundred different responses. Everything from, "I'm trying to clear my hips faster in order to generate more clubhead speed" to, "I'm just trying to hit the ball." Everybody's out there trying something, and that's the whole problem.

Forget about it. On the golf course you have to let things happen and allow yourself to score well. Consciously trying almost never works, so you have to break out of the trying mode and get into a trusting mode. Trying to hit the ball straight almost always leads to a bigger slice. Trying to out drive your friends leads to weak mis-hits. So forget about trying. If you want to score well just keep it simple, make your best effort on every shot, and move on. Have fun. In *Going Low* Dr. Patrick Cohen writes, "If you try too hard to shoot a low score, you make golf more complicated. Great players score their best when they make golf simple."

It's sad, but in all our research for this book Andy and I found hardly any references at all to having fun on the golf course. Most players and instructors are so intent on improving scores and fine tuning swings they've forgotten that they're playing a game. The obsession with numbers and mechanics drastically reduces the fun of the game and turns it into a task or a chore instead of a privilege.

In the British Isles they have a different mindset. Over there, match play is the most common form of competition and you see guys picking up their balls quite regularly. The emphasis isn't on measuring up to a handicap or posting a score, it's on beating the other guys in the group. It's a game of friendly competition that demands creativity, and yes, a little physical exertion. You won't find anybody riding around Muirfield or St. Andrews in a golf cart.

So the next time you're standing on the first tee, forget about everything else and make up your mind to have fun. Even if that first drive sails 75 yards out of bounds, you can still have fun. And remember, there's a reason it's called playing golf. It's supposed to be play, not work.

THE AMOUNT OF FUN IS DIRECTLY PROPORTIONATE TO YOUR EXPECTATIONS.

Jack Nicklaus once said the biggest problem most amateurs have is an unrealistic evaluation of their own talent. Basically, you think you're superman and you attempt shots that would be tough even for a tour pro. Like the low, 2-iron stinger that Tiger Woods has made famous. The elevator-like trajectory of a Phil Mickelson lob. The high draw around a tree, over the water and onto the green. Forget about it. Unless you're practicing those shots 20 hours a week it's almost impossible to execute them on the course when you need to.

Let's say you need to hit a big hook around a tree. Chances are, you'll over think it, even if you've done it before on the driving range. You get so wrapped up in the technicalities of hitting a hook, you miss it completely. If you're having a lucky day you might make it out to the fairway. If not, you end up in worse shape than when you started, kicking yourself for making a bad decision.

> **"There's no such thing as a golfer playing over his head. A hot streak is simply a glimpse of a golfer's true potential."**
> **-Dr. Bob Rotella**

You'll have a lot more fun in the long run if you're honest with yourself and just stick to the shots you know you can hit. Keep it simple. Know your strengths and accept the fact that you can't play a 240 yard 2-iron over water.

All the gurus of sports psychology agree that expectations of any kind are your worst enemy on the golf course. Expectations are inherently judgmental. You judge your last shot, your recent scores, the current conditions or whatever, and you set your expectations accordingly. If you're coming off a really great round, and you expect to duplicate those results, you'll probably be disappointed. If you bogie the first few holes or lose a ball, your dwindling expectations for the round will often become a self-fulfilling prophecy.

Great players simply don't go there. When tour pros go low they don't start out expecting to shoot 62. They know they have the potential to, but they don't get ahead of themselves by thinking about future outcomes.

Just listen to what they say in the post-round interviews. They almost always talk about how they "stayed in the present" and most will admit that it was lots of fun. Of course it's fun making birdies and eagles! But what came first, the low score or the part about having fun? We're convinced it's the mindset that allows the low scores to happen. And one thing's for sure: If you're not having fun you're not going to score very well.

As a consumer, you're always asking yourself "what's in it for me?" If you choose to spend your valuable time reading this book, what will you get out of it?" Why should you choose one golf course over another? If you fork over $400 for a new driver, what's in it for you?

The same thing could be asked of your golf game. What do you get out of the game? If you spend five hours of your day chasing a little white ball around a really big lawn, what's the take-away? What benefits do you derive from that, and does your pleasure depend entirely on the final score?

Timothy Gallwey says that any human activity offers three types of benefits: I. The rewards that come from performance, or the external results of the activity. 2. Benefits produced by the experience of performing the activity. 3. Benefits from the learning or growth that takes place during the activity. Three different types of satisfaction, and two out of three have nothing to do with scoring or performance.

Unfortunately, there are way too many people out there who get absolutely no satisfaction out of a round that's just mediocre from a scoring standpoint. They don't enjoy the experience of being out there with their friends. They don't learn anything from their mistakes. And they go away discouraged, frustrated, or worse.

Forget about it. If you fit into this category — and most people do at least some of the time — commit to making every round a learning experience. You'll have a lot more fun and there will be less pressure to perform well, which ironically results in better scoring. Plus, you'll gain something even from the bad rounds.

You can learn a lot by replaying any round in your head. If you look at it objectively, most of your mistakes will make complete sense. "Well, I stood around for 15 minutes on that tee, and when it was finally my turn I didn't go through my normal routine and yanked it left." You'll know when your thinking interfered with a shot, and when it didn't. You'll see, quite clearly, how a bad decision resulted in a miss, or how a good shot came to be. In a bad round, the good shots stand out quite vividly.

When your focus shifts away from performance-based benefits, you'll get much more enjoyment out of the game. For some people it's a profound eye opener. All of a sudden they start celebrating the minor victories and start noticing the little things that had escaped them for years. They begin to really appreciate golf course architecture. They make new friends and create deeper, lasting relationships with the people they've played with for years. And coincidentally, many people begin playing better, too.

As Bob Rotella says you can't control the results, but you can control your thoughts. So forget about scoring once in a while. Put aside your expectations and devote yourself to having a positive learning experience, regardless of the outcome. Sure, scoring well is always fun, but it shouldn't be the only thing that drives you.

MINIMIZE YOUR MISTAKES BY WINNING THE BATTLE WITH YOURSELF.

Every time you set foot on the golf course there's an epic battle that takes place. It's not between you and your opponents. It's not you versus the golf course or you versus the elements. It you versus your biggest nemesis — yourself.

In *The Inner Game Of Golf*, Timothy Gallwey refers to these two separate entities as "Self 1 and Self 2." Self 1 is the enemy, constantly analyzing things and interfering with the natural physical ability of Self 2.

Dr. Richard Coop refers to the conflict between the "analyzer" and the "integrator." "You don't have to have a split personality to be a good golfer, but it helps. One is serious, precise, analytical — the do it by the numbers person. The integrator is the golfer who swings the club — or more accurately, allows it to be swung without over-controlling it."

Bob Rotella distinguishes between the training self and the trusting self. Some players would simply say it's the conscious versus the subconscious. The Ego versus the Id. Left brain versus right brain.

Just for fun, we're going to call it "The Brain" versus "The Player." The good news is, there's a little bit of The Player in all of us. How do you think a 30-handicapper makes a hole in one? At any given moment, any adult with even below-average strength and coordination has the physical ability to hit a perfect golf shot. But to do that The Player has to win the battle against The Brain. Trust over doubt. Intuition over intellect.

> **"For the majority of golfers it is the mind, not the body, that is causing most of the errors and costing so many strokes. "**
> **–Dr. Richard Coop**

The first step in winning the battle is to embrace it. Accept the fact that the war is going to wage on, no matter what you do. It's human nature. The Brain is a formidable foe and he will always be there, lurking, looking for ways to sabotage a perfectly satisfying round of golf. So just be aware of it, and recognize it for what it is. Sometimes The Brain will get the better of you, sometimes he won't. And it doesn't matter how good you get, this battle will always be an integral part of the game. In fact, it's this very fight that makes golf the most addictive game in the world.

The second step is to develop enough self awareness to know the enemy when he's sneaking up behind you. The Brain can take on many different forms, depending on your personality. For some people he's violent and angry. For others he's sloppy and lackadaisical. But there are some common traits that I'm sure you'll recognize.

Compared to The Player, The Brain is noisy and obstinate. He's that nagging voice in your head that shouts "Don't hit it over there you idiot!" "Don't three putt again," Don't, don't, don't, don't! Forget about it.

The Brain lives with his eyes glued to the rearview mirror. He reacts to the results of every shot — especially the bad ones — and gets all emotional on you. He is the guy who remembers every little tip you ever heard and applies them at the most inopportune times. He's the only opponent you'll ever have that can ruin your putting stroke and plant seeds of doubt where none ever existed.

The Player, on the other hand, lives in the moment and embraces the potential of every shot. And he's good, too. When The Player is running the show you have better feel, smoother tempo and a sharper eye for the target. Your senses are heightened, and the ball actually follows orders for a change.

The Brain is egotistical. He wants to show everyone how good he is and prove that the double bogie on the last hole was just a fluke. His entire identity is wrapped up in his ability to play golf according to some very specific expectations.

The Player is fearless. He doesn't care what other people think of him, and he never judges another person by his scorecard. He has nothing to prove.

The Brain is cunning and deceitful. Sometimes he disguises himself as a positive attitude, like, "wow, that was a good par. If I just make one more on this last hole, I'll beat my personal best."

The Player has the freedom and the spirit of the child within. He is creative, intuitive and highly adept at handling adversity. If The Brain interferes with your tee shot and you end up in the long grass behind a tree, it's The Player that gets you out. Seve Ballesteros used to have such a high degree of trust in The Player he didn't care if he drove it in the rough. He always knew he could find a way out. He was a master of improv.

The last thing you need to understand about this battle is that you're only going to win a small percentage of the time. (This is a tough one to accept for all those over-achieving control freaks who play golf.) Most of the 80 or 90 shots you take in a round will not be played purely by The Player. Interference from The Brain will influence most shots in some way, even for the pros. It's just a matter of how much and how often. As Timothy Gallwey said, "performance is a function of ability minus interference."

So the question is, how can you minimize that interference? How can you take everything you've learned, forget about it, and just play.

MAKE THE BRAIN AN ALLY, THEN DISTRACT HIM LONG ENOUGH TO HIT YOUR SHOT.

The Brain is like a meddling double agent in the mental battle that is golf. You have to use that side of your brain to get information, to analyze data, and to make decisions. Then, when it comes time for the mission, you have to occupy him with some menial tasks while The Player executes the shot.

Luckily, you only have to distract The Brain long enough to swing the club. Just a few seconds of mental silence is all it takes. Unfortunately, for most people it's almost impossible to silence The Player completely and think of nothing, even for a few seconds. So if you can't clear your head, what do you do?

> "You play your best golf when you plan with your head and then play with your heart... The intuitive mind is what gets control. It's the expert at running the body and it exerts beautiful control over the tiniest muscle movements if it's not interfered with by the thinking mind."
> **—Joseph Parent, *Zen Golf***

Most good players make up some sort of mental swing key that they can focus on. "Straight back and straight through." "Turn back and finish strong." "Clear the right side." Seems like everyone has something a little different.

Swing keys can be a good diversion. They give The Brain the technical input it always seems to need, but they can also cause problems. Most swing keys — by definition — are based on theories and mechanics. They're just technical reminders of what to do with the swing and the very nature of them invites more thinking. And as you well know, the less thinking the better. Not only that, swing keys often involve a lot of negative thinking like "Don't slide the hips, "or "Don't get stuck on the back foot." Forget about it. You absolutely cannot score well when you're thinking about mechanics. So if you're going to use a swing key, keep it positive and feel-oriented. Not technical.

Quite honestly, we don't even like the term "swing key." Instead, try "shot thought." A shot thought is not just a general idea, it's specific to the situation at hand. It's not mechanical, but tactile in nature. And it's totally target oriented.

In a perfect world you wouldn't even need a shot thought. You could just turn off The Brain at the flick of a switch and play the shot with nothing but peace and harmony on your mind. It's not going to happen. The Brain won't give up that easily, so you're going to need some kind of good diversion or distraction. Something that will occupy The Brain while The Player plays the shot. Remember, you don't hit the ball with your head.

For visually oriented people, words alone don't do the trick. You need pictures or images in order to trigger the right kind of thinking. For some people an audio diversion works well. Humming a tune as you play a shot has a way of engaging the creative side of your brain — the same side where The Player resides. It's also helpful for smoothing out your tempo. Simple mnemonic devises are also good. Just hear the sounds in your head. "Bingo bango bongo." "The tick tock." "turn-return." Whatever. It just needs to be something that resonates with you.

Another good strategy is to focus all your analytic energy on the target. Just concentrate on all the details of where the ball is going. Let The Brain latch onto that thought while your body handles the shot.

Timothy Gallwey recommends thinking of something else entirely. Develop a train of thought that involves something related to golf, but much simpler than the swing. Associative thinking, it's called. For instance, you could occupy your mind by thinking of the simple act of tapping in a six-inch putt. What could be easier? Instead of worrying about the water on the right and the towering fir trees on the left, think of how you would tap in a six inch putt.

Andy says routine is the most effective distraction for many of his students. The idea is to let The Brain obsess over every detail of the grip, aim, and stance. Just forget about any swing thoughts and focus on the step-by-step process and the rhythm of it so you execute the routine the same way, at the same pace, every time. That way you won't be thinking technical thoughts when it's time to pull the trigger.

But it's not easy. The Brain always wants to assert himself into the equation. Even the best pros sometimes find themselves totally out of their rhythm. So when you practice you have to train yourself to focus on the process, not the results. The goal is not to hit a great shot, the goal is simply to just stick to the routine. Routine and rhythm. If you have those two things dialed in, good shots will follow quite naturally.

The next time you're at the driving range stop and pay attention to your routine. Forget about the results for a minute and focus all your attention on the habits you have leading up to the swing. Remember, awareness is the only goal. If you don't know what you do, how can you do it the same way every time?

If you determine that there's really no rhyme nor reason to your routine, that's okay. Most people have never given this a second thought, and it's easy enough to make something up.

Andy has helped me streamline my routine significantly. And

every time we get together he checks to make sure I'm still doing it the same way at the same pace. I'm a naturally right-brained person and my routine is designed to fit my personality. For me, standing over the ball and taking several looks at the target isn't a good idea. My swing is fairly quick, like Nick Price's, and my routine needs to match that. But everyone is different.

Experiment a little until you discover a process that you think you could work with. For instance, try taking your practice swings while standing behind the ball, looking at the target. Take a deep, cleansing breath just before you swing. Try it with a waggle. Do whatever it takes to get relaxed and comfortable, then turn the steps into a little routine that works right into making a good swing. And don't over-complicate things.

It's going to take a few practice sessions to come up with a step-by-step process that feels natural for you. As you begin to piece together something that resembles a routine, say the steps out loud a few times. Feel the rhythm of it. Hear the words and take time to write them down. And let The Brain go to work on it. If he wants to analyze every little piece of the pre-shot routine, that's quite all right. It's a lot better than taking the swing apart piece by piece.

The more you practice that routine, the more natural your swing will be. While The Brain is busy keeping the routine consistent, The Player will start hitting shots that you never knew you had. And before you know it, your scores will start going down. But there's a diabolical twist to all this. As your habits improve — and your preshot routine gets more and more ingrained in your sub-conscious — the opportunities for The Brain to interfere actually increase. In other words, when the routine becomes so routine that you don't think about it, then The Brain is free to insert destructive, mechanical thoughts. Again, that's why you have to stay aware of — and focused on — the process. You have to practice the routine regularly, and constantly remind yourself to forget about swing mechanics and focus on routine. That's what will make the biggest difference in your game.

ON THE GOLF COURSE, FEAR IS THE ROOT OF ALL EVIL.

Some days, this game seems ridiculously easy. Anyone who's played for some time knows the feeling. Those are the days when you're winning the battle between The Brain and The Player. You're playing in a state of heightened awareness but somehow you're able to maintain a sort of detached objectivity. You're perfectly balanced between being too careful and being careless. You're carefree and loving it.

As you approach the ball you engage The Brain to assess the conditions and size up the shot. There's no fear of missing. No second guessing. Your routine flows naturally and once you're over the ball you simply switch into automatic and let your unconscious self — The Player — swing the club. It's what some people refer to as "playing out of your head" or "getting out of your own way." With little or no interference from The Brain, you're quite able to play the game way beyond your expectations.

So why are those rounds so few and far between? Many books — and thousands of therapy sessions — have been devoted to that question. But we think it all boils down to fear. Deep down we're afraid of what others are going to think if we miss an easy putt or slice a tee shot into a house.

> "Courage is a necessary quality in all champions. But an athlete cannot be courageous without first being afraid."
>   **-Joseph Parent**

Forget about it. That's The Brain talking, and he's not being very rational. It's The Brain that attaches his personal worth to the outcome of his golf game, not The Player. It's The Brain that's scared of reliving past failures. It's The Brain that harbors all the doubt. He's the one with the trust issues. If you look at it that way, and accept the fact that The Brain is the fearful one, it'll be much easier to play through it.

Whether it's the fear of failure, the fear of success, or some rare phobia of birdies, don't deny it or try to fight it. Acknowledge it. Say to yourself, "Okay Brain, I know you're really scared of going in that lake again. Last time I did that I made a triple bogie. That really stunk." Then remind yourself that The Brain is not the one who's going to play the shot. You can't hit the ball with your head. The fear is real, but it does not reside in The Player. He's fearless, remember. If you just go through your routine, employ your diversionary tactics and let The Player do his work, fear won't affect the shot.

When you're afraid, you get tense. And as you know, muscle tension can throw your swing off faster than you can yell "fore." But separating your two selves will help maintain an objective attitude toward your fears and, consequently, help you stay relaxed.

Deepak Chopra says "Winning is passion with detachment." And that's one of the traits that all great players share. They're able to stay objective enough to accept their bad shots and move on, without trying to correct things. This slightly removed perspective or self-image might be the only thing that keeps the touring pros sane. They can see their fear without getting caught up in it emotionally. They can let go without worrying about results. They can harness the power of The Brain and then turn the control over to The Player.

FOR LOWER SCORES, START SHARPENING YOUR SHORT GAME.

You want stats, we'll give you stats. Dave Pelz says that 68 percent of your shots during a typical round are not full shots. Specifically, 43 percent are putts and 25 percent are chips, pitches or bunker shots. Of course the numbers vary a little depending on your ability, but the fact remains: The short game is where tournaments are won and lost. It's where the average golfer makes the biggest mistakes and throws away the most strokes. Yet it's the least taught and the least practiced part of the game.

If you don't believe it, just look at all the old guys who can beat the pants off you without driving it more than 220 yards. Look at the people who win club championships on a regular basis.

It's not the big hitters. It's almost always someone who can chip and putt better than everyone else. Hillary Lunke won the 2003 U.S. Women's Open without hitting anything longer than 225 yards. She just kept it in the fairway and played flawlessly on and around the greens.

The history books are full of stories like that. So forget about out-driving your competition and start polishing your short game. This is one of the most basic tenants of the Forget About It mindset.

> **"Golf is not a game of great shots, it's a game of the most misses. Those who win make the smallest mistakes."**
> **—Gene Littler**

Most people neglect the short game simply because those little wedge shots don't provide the same thrill as hitting a driver. There's no adrenaline rush. Anybody can learn to chip and putt.

Forget about it. If you're going to play well you need to find something gratifying in making those delicate little shots. You have to thrive on getting up and down out of bunkers. You have to love the feeling of a well-struck putt just as much as a well-struck drive. Rather than lamenting the fact that you missed the green you have to choose to enjoy the challenge of the recovery shot. Ya gotta love those pars or bogies that you make by chipping it close or draining a clutch putt.

Short game success hinges on making smart decisions and hitting the type of shot that has the best chance of success. It's the short shots that invite the most kibitzing from The Brain, so it's important to keep things simple. As a general rule of thumb, you want to get the ball rolling as soon as possible. So when you're assessing a short chip, always ask yourself, "can I roll it?"

The best club for that shot is the putter. In Scotland they use the putter from all sorts of weird places. At Bandon Dunes on the Oregon Coast it's not uncommon to see someone putting from 50 or 60 yards out. And in Texas the putter is used so frequently it's actually called the Texas wedge. Experiment around the green with your putter; you'll be amazed how successful you can be from all kinds of different lies. About the only time you don't want a putter is when you're dealing with long greenside rough.

If you can't roll the ball with your putter you might try your 3-wood. Just choke up all the way to the bottom of the grip and make a nice, putter-like stroke. The loft of the 3-wood is often just enough to carry a couple feet of rough.

Unless you're going to practice religiously don't get side tracked experimenting with all sorts of fancy Phil Michelson flop shots. Forget about it. The more choices you have the more indecision you'll experience and the more you'll miss-hit shots. Just get the ball on the green and get it rolling.

If you're off the green and you can't use your putter, another good option is to play what we call the 9-iron putt. It's a particularly good choice if your ball is buried in thick grass. First you have to change your setup dramatically: Move the ball way back in your stance and set the shaft almost straight up and down, like you're going to hit it off the toe of the club. Then you can use a good, firm putting stroke and it'll squirt out of that tough little lie with some topspin roll. It isn't difficult as long as the setup is correct, but the distance control takes some getting used to. We don't recommend trying it unless you have someone who can demonstrate it first.

The third choice for greenside shots is the standard chip that pops up and lands softly. A chip shot is useful when you have to fly over a bunker or a sprinkler head. Again, we believe it's best to keep things simple. Rather than playing a variety of different clubs just practice chipping with your sand wedge. You'll have a better feel for how far the ball's going and there won't be any seeds of doubt concerning club selection. If you want a low chip, just go back to the 9-iron putt we just described.

A lot of people get totally confused when they read tips on chipping. I know I did. One magazine article says you should chip like you putt, while the next magazine prescribes a definite chipping technique with a slight breaking of the wrists. Which is it? The general perception is that you have to choose one method or the other. Forget about it. They're both good shots in certain instances, you just have to know when to play the basic chip shot and when to play the 9-iron putt.

We could write another entire book on the art of the bunker shot. The pros make it look impossibly easy, but for most people it's the most dreaded shot on the course. And to make matters worse, instruction books make it much more difficult than it needs to be. They tell you to open the clubface, set your feet into the sand, pretend that you're sitting in a chair, swing along the line of your feet, hinge your wrists, set the club, hit behind the ball, put the weight on your left side, take the club up sharply, on and on and on. There's so much stuff to remember it's mind numbing. No wonder so many bunker shots end up across the green or in the same bunker where they started. You can't possibly be thinking about all those things and then expect The Player to take over. It's not going to happen.

The best advice we could give you on this shot is to get a lesson. Just get with your instructor and spend one hour in a bunker. You'll be amazed at how easy it really is once you have the fundamental setup figured out. From there it's just a matter of swinging freely, without thinking about how to hit the shot and without hesitating. You may not sink a lot of these shots like the pros do, but you'll get it up there around the hole and leave yourself a good chance of making the putt.

ON THE THINGS YOU CAN AND CAN'T CONTROL.

If you're going to play a lot of golf, you need to understand something. A lot of what happens out there is completely out of your control. A gust of wind kicks up just as you're playing an important approach shot. Your drive splits the fairway and ends up in a nasty divot that no one bothered to repair. The Brain kicks in just as you're about to hit a bunker shot. Stuff happens. That's golf.

If you let every little misfortune affect you, the game's not going to be much fun. You all know people like that. The minute they hit a couple bad shots they start beating themselves up so badly that no one wants to be around them. Some whine and moan. Some cuss and throw clubs. Others just behave like spoiled little brats, as if a low score is a God-given right that's somehow been stolen from them. Try caddying for awhile, you'll experience every type imaginable.

Just forget about it. No matter how hard you try, or how long you practice, there will be random bizarre occurrences on the golf course. Both good and bad.

> **"Don't play the game. Let the game play you."**
> **–Deepak Chopra**

As Bob Rotella says, you can't control the outcome of the game, but you can control your thoughts, your attitude and your outlook. When you're not playing quite as well as you'd like, you can choose to have a good time anyway, or you can choose to be miserable.Usually this choice is a reflection of the player's personality. If he's an old curmudgeon in life, he's probably going to be miserable on the golf course too. And vice versa.

Many people point to Fred Couples as a model of self control. He seems unflappable. He just kinda lumbers around the golf course with the same carefree appearance whether he's making birdies or not. But that's Freddy. He's more laid back than a aging Adirondack chair.

Sergio Garcia, on the other hand, has that same Spanish bravado that Seve Ballesteros had. Compared to Freddy, he's a firecracker waiting to go off. For Sergio to control his emotions would be contradictory to his nature and counterproductive. His passion is what makes him great, and it's healthy to let that passion show through on the golf course.

Peter Jacobsen's another good example. Lee Trevino. Arnold Palmer. They're all tremendously popular players because of their friendly, outgoing personalities. None of them would have been successful if they had been all business on the golf course.

So be true to yourself. If you're the strong silent type in life, by all means put on your David Duval glasses and go do your thing. If you're kind of a clown, that's okay, too. Don't try to be someone you're not just because you're on a golf course.

Another important point to remember is that golf is essentially a social endeavor. There will almost always be other people in your group who you have to interact with, and they don't want to hear about all your misery and woe. They have their own challenges. So if you are a grumpy old man at heart, you might want to just forget about it and stick with fishing or some other solitary pastime.

6
THE FORGET-ABOUT-IT GUIDE
TO PUTTING

"Good putting is at best a fleeting blessing. Here today, gone tomorrow. So I think we waste time and energy trying to perfect a putting stroke... Too much worrying about details of how the hitting is done is fatal to good putting."

—BOBBY JONES

Nothing messes with your head more perversely than a simple putt — missed. Just one or two in an otherwise satisfying round of golf can trigger astronomical amounts of analysis, frustration and experimentation. In fact, nowhere is the binge and purge problem more pervasive than in putting.

For many players the ups and downs of putting can turn into a sickening roller coaster ride. The minute they miss a couple putts they start looking for a fix, usually in the form of a new putter or a new putting method. They start analyzing and overanalyzing their stroke and pretty soon, it's nothing but trial and error. Mostly error. Round and around they go.

I've been on that merry-go-round for years, and it's not fun. Instead of just taking a putting lesson I spent years trying to figure it out on my own. I read everything I could get my hands on about putting. I worked on getting my backswing the same length as my follow-through and my putts precisely 16 inches past the cup. I experimented with every method, every grip, and every type of putter on the market. At one time, after reading an entire book about the visual incongruities of putting, I seriously considered Sam Snead's side-saddle approach. I even invented my own overlap grip that will undoubtedly be sweeping the nation the minute this book hits the streets.

The whole thing was a disaster. In fact, the decision to change my putting method was the single worst thing I've ever done to my golf game. It was the beginning of a long, downward spiral that led into the pits of hell commonly known as the yips.

If you're not familiar with the yips it's when your mind gets so cluttered your body simply refuses to function. I'd get over a putt and seize up so bad they'd have to bring out the portable defibrillators to get me moving again. When I did manage to make contact with the ball it looked like 5,000 volts were surging through my fingers causing all the muscles in my body to contract at once. I had no feel whatsoever for lag putts — only one in five were stopping within six feet of the hole, and I could easily miss a simple five footer by two or more feet in either direction. And the shorter the putt, the worse it got.

There were many low points — dips so deep and depressing I thought I'd never come out of it. At one point I gave up on the club entirely and just started putting with my driver, or blading 'em with my wedge. Anything to avoid standing over a three-footer with that infernal putter in my hand. I couldn't possibly play in my usual men's club events — not when partners were involved. The only games I dared enter were an occasional 4-man scramble.

That's where I first played golf with Andy. He was our ringer in a scramble where mulligans were bought and sold almost as frequently as beers. He coached us through the round, helped us plot our strategy on each hole and schooled us on all our putts.

But even with Andy's help in the pressure-free environment of a scramble, I putted terribly. My yips were painfully obvious to everyone in the group. At one point Andy politely asked why I chose the belly putter.

Well, uhhhh… good question. I didn't tell him it was an act of desperation. A last straw.

"It works for Vijay Singh and Freddy Couples, " I said lamely.

"Yea, but does it work for you?"

The seed was planted and I obviously needed help, so a few days later — after golfing for 30 years — I finally broke down and met Andy for a putting lesson.

There's definitely a stigma attached to spending valuable time with a golf pro on the putting green. It's like proclaiming to the world you're a complete idiot. "Hey look at me, I don't even have enough coordination to roll this little ball ten feet, much less 300-yards down a narrow fairway. What a loser!"

Everyone knows how simple putting really is. Dave Pelz has concluded that walking is 100 times harder than putting, so if you can walk around the course without tripping over your own two feet, you ought to be able to putt. But that's no consolation for those of you who have ever sweated over an easy three-footer.

The truth is, you make putting much harder than it really is simply by thinking about it too darn much. You sabotage yourself by using a putter that doesn't suit your body type and your technique. You complicate it by analyzing the putting stroke to death. You compound your problems by trying to teach yourself every new method that comes along. And you make it hard by neglecting the fundamentals of putting.

Forget about it. If you're struggling with your putting you're thinking about it way too much. You're probably trying to figure out what method to use and what putter to buy with no real guidance or accurate feedback. And without help you'll be condemned to a life of experimentation, false hope and frustration. The more you read and the more methods you try, the worse it's going to get. Over-analysis of the stroke is, by far, the most common cause of the yips. You don't want to fall into that trap, believe me.

You can save yourself a lot of misery just by swallowing your pride and spending a few hours with a good putting coach. It's not like a full-swing lesson where things sometimes get worse before they get better. Even one lesson with a good instructor can produce immediate — and lasting — improvement on the putting green. (As long as you don't get preoccupied with the mechanics of it.)

Andy didn't teach me to putt, I've known that since I was 10. He just reminded me that I could. He showed me how simple it really is and he taught me how to practice putting without letting The Brain get in the way.

Thanks to Andy I recently sank a downhill, 15 footer for eagle. And what's more, I made a testy six-footer for par on the last hole to tie that match. I still have some bad habits that creep back in occasionally, but I'm not yipping it anymore. I'm not on that roller coaster of experimentation and I'm not putting with a disturbing sense of wonder. I don't wonder if I'm lined up correctly. I don't wonder if I have the right putter in my hands. I don't wonder if my setup is correct or my stroke is fundamentally sound. Thanks to a few simple putting lessons I can forget about all those nagging mechanical thoughts and just swing the clubhead with confidence. And that's the closest thing I've ever encountered to a cure for the yips.

We put this chapter at the end of our book because everything you've learned so far applies to putting. (If you skipped straight to this chapter, turn back now.) Equipment is important, as is a good coach. If you're not careful, learning can be overwhelming. How you practice is more important than how much you practice. And most of all, the battle between your ears is at its peak when you're on the putting green.

What's more, while researching this book we discovered a pattern that Andy's follows when teaching people to get over the yips. First, they put mechanics out of their mind and find their own, natural putting method. Second, they fine tune the fundamentals of that method. And finally, they train themselves to trust it.

I've found my natural way, that's the easy part. Forgetting and trusting are a lot tougher. Over the years I developed the bad habit of thinking about the stroke all the time, on every stinking putt, and breaking that habit is not easy. Dave Pelz says if you've been yipping it'll take 20,000 good putts to ingrain a new habit. So I have to continue to practice, without worrying about mechanics. And when my jerky old swing shows up, as it will occasionally, I know it's not my stroke that's the problem. It's just me, over thinking things again.

TO FIND YOUR NATURAL METHOD YOU HAVE TO FORGET ABOUT MECHANICS.

Forty years ago there weren't really any alternatives to the traditional method of putting. With the notable exception of Sam Snead, people just never even considered putting any other way. (Sam Snead experimented with croquet-style until the USGA banned it. Then he went with a side-saddle approach that never quite caught on with anyone else.)

But in the last 20 years, hundreds of new putting methods have popped up. You can use the Langer grip, the claw grip, the Arnold Palmer grip or even the Furgurson grip, if you like. You can also fiddle around with the length of your putter, from a back-breaking 28 inches to the chin-high 70 incher and anything in between. There are belly putters, chin putters, chest putters. It's only a matter of time till somebody introduces the crotch putter to the general public.

> "While putting is the one phase of the game of golf in which the individual is permitted to indulge himself in all kinds of freak ideas and weird mannerisms, I still like to putt the natural way. "
> **–Sam Snead**

Forget about it. If you're always experimenting with different methods of putting you'll be caught in a constant state of analysis. You'll never be able to switch it off and rely on your right-brain instincts. The Brain will always be getting in the way.

My search for a putting method began with what I learned as a kid. Bend over like Jack Nicklaus. Elbows out. Lock the wrists. Take the putter straight back — just a little ways — and straight through with a long follow-through. It was solid on slow, straight putts, but it didn't hold up well on undulating, bentgrass greens. Overall, I was streaky but good until I decided to give up my old Nicklaus method and try something new. That's when I got really bad.

Instead of finding my own, natural method I tried to apply a Vulcan mind probe to my putting stroke. For some reason I felt compelled to take a thoroughly analytical, binge-and-purge approach to my putting. I started experimenting with all sorts of putting grips, methods and secrets. I analyzed every nuance of every method. I read books and researched the theories of all the best putters. I even had a golf hole cut in the floor of my office.

At least a dozen times I thought I had it all figured out, only to be thwarted by another dismal performance on the course. Each poor performance led to more analysis. And the further I delved into it, the more mechanical my putting stroke became. No matter how hard I tried it just kept getting worse and worse until the day that I stopped, cold turkey, and took a lesson from Andy.

Andy had only one goal for my first putting lesson: He just wanted to see what I could do if I wasn't locked in a constant state of analysis. So he didn't waste any time talking about methods, he simply handed me a novel new putter and said here, hit some with this.

Easier said than done. The club was called the PutterBall — basically, a putter with a lead ball for a clubhead, no bigger than a golf ball. It would take all my skill just to make contact between the club and the ball, and if I mis-hit it by one millimeter the ball would go shooting off into left field.

I took a couple practice swings, just to get the feel for the extra weight of the club. Then I stepped up to the ball and stroked several putts straight into the cup with a putter that leaves virtually no room for error. It was a miracle. All I was trying to do was hit the ball square, and somehow it was finding the hole. Even though I was a little nervous there wasn't a hint of a yip. I was so intent on proving that I could hit the ball, I didn't have a chance to analyze anything. There were no thoughts of rocking the shoulders or firming up the wrists. No fiddling with my grip. No freezing up. I just wanted to hit the ball, and hit the ball I did. Better than I had in years.

It was obvious that I could putt — I just wasn't letting it happen with the belly putter. "Just find your own natural way," Andy said. "Forget about how everyone else is doing it and just do what feels natural to you. The simpler the better. It has to be a no-brainer. You have to be comfortable enough with the basic technique to just stand up to the ball and pull the trigger. Otherwise, you'll always be thinking about the mechanics of your method."

Five minutes into my first putting lesson it was obvious that I had to give up the belly putter and go back to something more natural. Once I quit fiddling with umpteen different methods and found my own, natural style everything fell into place. I ended up with a simple, traditional putting style that allows my natural ability to come through. It's a style inspired more by Bobby Locke than Jack Nicklaus.

South African Bobby Locke, four-time British Open Champion, is often considered one of the best putters to ever live. (In 1946 he beat Sam Snead head-to-head in 10 out of 12 exhibition matches.) His goal was to develop a putting stroke and routine that was as similar as possible to the way he played all his other shots. "The fewer variations in one's technique, the more consistent one becomes," he said.

So forget about experimenting with various putting methods. Try following Locke's advice and start playing your putts more like your other shots. That's what I'm doing.

Ever since my first lesson with Andy I've eliminated all the variations in my setup and my stroke — I'm not all hunched over. I don't have the grip of the putter imbedded in my belly. I'm not copying anyone or forcing myself to putt one way or another. I'm just doing what feels natural for me. I just address the ball and swing the putter without thinking about the stroke at all.

That's the first thing you have to learn if you're going to beat the yips — how to forget about mechanics. In fact, you have to forget about the putting stroke entirely. If you're thinking about the stroke — whether it's going straight back or if the putter's square at impact or whatever — you'll never find your natural way, and you'll never stop yipping. Plain and simple. You can't think and putt at the same time. You can only think and yip.

The Mayo Clinic has actually done studies on this phenomenon. Results show that people with the yips exhibit an inordinate amount of activity in the left hemisphere of the brain while putting. They're over-thinking it. On the other hand, crack putters seem to redirect their brain function just before they putt. They sort of turn off their left brain — the analytical side — and just let the Player take over. In other words, they relax and let it happen.

Remember, you can't un-learn anything. All you can do is replace one habit with another. So if you've been using a traditional style for some time, it's going to take a lot of hard work and repetition to change to a claw grip or a belly putter. There will be a long period of discomfort before you ever get the feel of the new technique.

Vijay Singh has had considerable success with the belly putter, but he's one of the hardest working guys on tour. Singh devoted hundreds of hours to practicing the new method. Most golfers don't take a hundred practice putts in an entire year.

If you've been struggling with which putting method to use, our best advice is to get some help. Save yourself a lot of heartache and get an expert opinion. If you don't, you'll just continue to question things. Every time you hit a cold streak you'll start wondering if you should change this or tweak that. And doubt is the kiss of death when it comes to putting.

GET COMFORTABLE WITH THE CLUB YOU'RE USING.

News flash: You don't have to have a perfect stroke to be a good putter. You don't have to hit every putt precisely the right speed for them to drop. You don't have to practice mechanics to get good. But you do have to be comfortable over the ball if you want a reasonable chance of making your fair share of putts.

Raymond Floyd says that playing comfortable is the best advice he can give anyone about golf. He believes it's the biggest factor in consistently getting the most from your game, and it's one of three traits that all good putters share.

So what, exactly does playing comfortable mean when it comes to putting? It means you're comfortable with the club you're using. You're comfortable with your natural method — be it traditional, left hand low, claw grip or whatever. You're comfortable with your read of the green, and finally, you're comfortable with your state of mind.

Let's take the club first. If you're going to be consistent on the greens you have to be totally comfortable with every aspect of the club you're using. You have to be comfortable with how the putter looks, how it feels and how it sounds.

Most people use an entirely subjective approach to choosing a putter. They simply find one that "feels good." But your sense of touch can betray you. There are literally thousands of different putters out there to choose from and many are crafted out of soft new metals and high-tech polymers that have a great feel to them. But that doesn't mean they're right for you.

For visually oriented people the look of the putter might be more important than the feel. If the putter doesn't look like it'll work, it won't. You'll never be comfortable with it. As a general rule the simpler the better when it comes to visual appeal. You don't want anything distracting you.

For other people the sound quality of a good, solid putt is also crucial. Some putters make a distinctive "clink" when you hit the ball, providing a significant amount of sensory feedback. Other putters, particularly those with polymer inserts in the face, will be much quieter, both to the ear and to the touch. Studies have shown that sound translates to feel. That is, the putters that sound nice and soft are also the ones that are perceived to have better feel.

The easiest way to avoid a self-defeating cycle of trial and error and get completely comfortable with your putter is to go through a dynamic clubfitting exercise similar to what I did with Andy. It's the only way you'll ever know for sure that your putter is well suited to your style of putting.

A few days after I passed Andy's little eye-hand coordination test with the Putterball we got together for a putting fitting. Andy showed up looking like a pool shark at a big money match. In his custom suitcase he had an infinite variety of shafts, hosels and putter heads to try out. Through a simple process of elimination he said he could find the one combination that's perfectly suited to my style of putting, my body type, my visual acuity and my sense of sense of feel.

Andy explained that proper putting alignment has as much to do with the putter as it does with the puttee. To prove it, he set-up a little test using a laser pen light as the target. With the laser beaming on the ball, he had me take a normal stance and aim the putter head at the target. Once in position, Andy took the ball away. The laser light reflected off a small mirror on the face of the putter and revealed that my aim was off considerably to the right. Hmmm. I thought for sure I was lined up, but there's no arguing with that laser.

Andy switched hosels and we tried again. This time the reflected light hit much closer to the target, but not quite on. So he kept trying different combinations of clubhead and hosel until we found one that lined up consistently at the target. I was amazed by the difference from one putter to the next, and it was plain to see that some putters simply didn't line up properly for me. It has to do with a lot of optical issues we can't begin to explore, but it's true.

When we were all done, I had a putter that was four degrees flat with an offset hosel, a round grip and no alignment aids whatsoever. (We found that lines etched on top of the putter head actually hurt my alignment, rather than helping it.) You can imagine the improvement in my confidence when I saw for certain that I was lining up the clubhead consistently at the intended target, instead of a foot to the right. For the first time in my life, nagging concerns about alignment disappeared. I finally stopped second guessing the putter itself and started rolling the ball in the hole using a natural swing and a natural setup. And you know what? It felt really, really good.

So forget about all the wishful thinking and experimentation. Work with a teaching pro who can build you a putter that's right for you in every regard. And once you've found one, stick with it. Resist the urge to try a new putter every time you have a bad day on the greens. As Harvey Penick said, "It's not your familiar old putter that has quit working, it's your mind that's avoiding performance for some reason."

My path to yiplessness started when I abandoned the belly putter and stopped working on my stroke. I went back to something much more traditional. More consistent with all my other clubs. And in the process I've eliminated a huge element of doubt that was contributing dramatically to my putting woes.

MAKE THE FUNDAMENTALS ROUTINE.

Let's assume, for a minute, that you've stopped experimenting and have settled on a putting method that feels completely natural to you. Let's also assume you have a putter that's specifically suited to your method. Not a club that just seems right, but one that is dialed in to all your individual quirks.

The next step is to ingrain the fundamentals of that method without getting too anal retentive about your stroke.

So what are the fundamentals of putting? Ask five different pros and you'll get five different answers to that. But all the opinions, writings and analysis can be boiled down into two thoughts: routine and rhythm. Every great tour player has a routine that he or she repeats every single time they putt. Without fail, they'll all attest to the importance of their unique routines, especially when the chips are down.

> "Putting seems to be a gift bestowed upon the young and innocent but is gradually and inexorably spirited away as players become more and more sophisticated and talented in other areas of the game."
> — Dave Pelz

By repeating a routine time after time they create a natural rhythm that becomes an automatic part of that routine. It's not a conscious rhythm, it's just how they do it. For some players it's a plodding, deliberate rhythm. For me, it's a little up-tempo, like my full swing. Routine produces rhythm. You can't have one without the other. And the more routine it is, the better your rhythm becomes.

Andy likes to call it the three R's. Routine plus Rhythm equals Reward. A good routine will take your mind off mechanics. It'll help you relax and make you more comfortable over the ball. And most importantly, it'll give you confidence under pressure.

I never realized how inconsistent my putting routine was until I sat down to write this chapter. I thought I did things pretty much the same way every time. I thought I knew exactly what it was, but when I tried to articulate it I had a very hard time. And when Andy saw it in print, he just laughed. If it were a graded assignment, he'd have given me an F.

First of all, my so-called routine wasn't nearly specific enough. Is it one practice swing or two? Is it a long look at the hole, or a quick glance? Does the process take three seconds or 30 seconds? I simply didn't know.

Secondly, my routine wasn't really my routine at all. It was more like wishful thinking than reality. Sometimes I'd do most of the steps in quick succession, and other times I'd do half the steps and take twice as long. Andy said he could always tell when I was going to hit a lousy putt because I'd fidget with my grip after I'd addressed the ball — definitely not part of the routine.

So with Andy's help, I revamped my routine completely. Without working at all on my actual putting stroke, I reinvented the way I way I putt. Now, when I practice putting, the only thing I think about is keeping the routine consistent.

The first step was to discover my natural rhythm. Andy timed me playing putts of various lengths and came up with an average. Then he showed me how much variation there was. Once we determined my natural tendencies we worked on simplifying the process and speeding things up a little. Given my history with the yips we wanted a routine that would minimize my chances of over-thinking things.

So now, once I've lined up the putt and I'm ready to address the ball, I recite this little mantra in my head: "Grip. Aim and stance. Look at the hole. Look at the ball. And swing." It's a six step process that should take six seconds. On the count of "one," I grip it. On "two," I put the putter down behind the ball and aim it at the preliminary target. Then on "three," without moving the putter or anything else, I set my feet. Right foot first, then left. On "four," I take a deliberate look at the hole. On "five," I look at a spot on the ground between my putter and the ball. On "six," I swing. It's not the fastest putting routine I've ever seen, but it's faster than most.

For me, following a step-by-step process means the difference between confidence and despair. By repeating those steps in my head I can occupy the Brain and turn the shot over to the Player — which, by the way, is quite capable of making putts. If you watch me putt you'd never know that once I get over the ball I go through six distinct steps. They all flow together into one nice, continuous movement, so I'm never frozen over the ball.

I've also realized that concentrating on the routine is the only thing that keeps my mind from jumping ahead. It keeps me "in the moment" as they say. Thinking of anything else would be thinking ahead, or dwelling on the past. Even thoughts as positive as the ball dropping into the hole could be construed as getting ahead of myself. As long as I focus only on executing my routine without hesitating along the way, I can forget about the stroke and putt pretty well. As Al Geiberger once said, "I perform best when I'm letting my subconscious mind hit the ball and my conscious mind is otherwise occupied."

Of course my routine is my routine, and it probably isn't perfect for you. Some people like to tap the putter on the ground three times just before they start the stroke. Some never set the club down at all. U.S. Open Champion Jim Furyk fakes like he's going to putt, and then backs away. Every time! As long as your routine relieves tension and gets you aimed properly at the target, it doesn't matter what the exact steps are. But the point is, you have to have the steps, and they need the same rhythm every time. The only way you'll ever accomplish that is by practicing the routine precisely, step by step, when you're not on the golf course.

By the way. A funny thing happened to me as I was practicing my new putting routine: My stroke improved immensely. Without ever thinking about it or working on it, my putting stroke improved. So the next time you're tempted to start fiddling with your putting stroke, just forget about it and shift your focus to the routine of putting. They are one in the same. You cannot separate the putting stroke from the rhythm and routine of putting.

I never could have recovered from the yips if I hadn't changed my putting routine. No way. Like most people with the yips, the harder I tried the longer it took me to putt, and the longer it took the worse the yips became.

Of course good routine also incorporates solid fundamentals. (It's not very productive if your routine involves aiming the clubhead five feet right every time.) So be sure to incorporate good posture, grip, aim and stance. If you have all the fundamental pieces in place you can focus all your attention on the routine and forget about everything else. The stroke will flow naturally from the rhythm of the routine, and before you know it, the sound of the ball falling in the up will also become part of your routine.

Don't Set Yourself Up For Failure.

There are far more variables in your putting set-up and pre-shot routine than there are in your putting stroke. The stroke's the easy part. That's why your routine is so important, because preparing to putt is a lot harder than actually putting.

If you want to putt consistently you need a routine that makes it easy to get the fundamentals right every time. The fundamental elements of good putting preparation are the same as they are for the full swing: grip, aim and stance.

The putting grip is totally a matter of personal preference. The simplest way is to just hold it like any other club in the bag. But you can hold it with the left hand low if it's comfortable. You can overlap or interlock. You can hold it in your fingertips or in your palms. Doesn't matter as long as you don't grip the club too firmly.

Many of the greatest putters say they barely hold onto the club at all, that's it's practically falling out of their hands on every putt. If you grip the putter too tightly you're going to create tension that will eventually cause a miss. Or more likely, a lot of misses. So forget about the death grip you have on it and forget about any "right or wrong" grip. Just find one that's comfortable for you and hold the putter as lightly as you can, without letting the clubhead twist in your hands. We like the advice that many little league coaches use for batting practice: "soft" hands.

Aim is a highly neglected fundamental, both in putting and in the full swing. People work for hours on their putting stroke without ever really thinking about good, consistent aim. You see it all the time on the practice green. Most people drop three or four balls on the green, and then start putting one after another without hardly looking up. They get totally fixated on striking the ball and neglect all the other preliminary steps.

The fact is, the average golfer doesn't have very good aim, even on short putts. Most people think they're aiming at the target, but when they're tested with a laser they're all over the place. So if you're going to improve it's absolutely essential to get some true feedback on your aim. You can try all sorts of different training aids and jury-rigged gadgets, or you can simplify the process and take a putting lesson. A good coach will spot alignment problems quite easily and will provide the accurate feedback you need to eliminate the guess-work from your putting set-up. Sometimes it's just the club that's throwing you off. He can also help you establish a little pre-shot routine to follow, and call you on it when you take short cuts.

When it comes to your putting stance the only thing that matters is comfort. Many great pros use a slightly open stance, claiming that it helps them see the line more clearly. You can go knock-kneed like Arnold Palmer, you can close your stance or put your feet perfectly together. Doesn't matter, as long as your shoulders are parallel to the target and you're not moving your body around during the swing.

Posture — which is another important part of your set-up — is also a matter of personal preference. Again, the simplest way to approach it is just like any other shot. Don't get all hunched over. Just take the same, natural stance you do on your short iron shots.

Two popular tips on posture really throw people off: "Let your arms hang down naturally," and "get your eyes right over the ball." Unless you love confusion, just forget about both of them.

There's a big difference between the arms hanging naturally and the arms hanging straight. Straight arms are tense. Relaxed arms have a little natural bend in them. (It's called an elbow.) When people hear these tips, and put the two together, they almost always bend over too much and try putting with their arms perfectly straight. Like Frankenstein.

Don't get hung up on the position of your eyes either. Granted, it may help your aim, but it's just not something you should think about. As long as you have nice, natural posture and aren't reaching drastically for the ball, your eyes will be aligned just fine.

Ball position is another important part of your setup. You can eliminate many of your miss-hits by simply playing the ball in the same spot every time. The ball should not be right in the middle of your stance, but slightly forward. Don't get too carried away though, and put the ball way up toward the left heel like you're playing a driver.

Most putts are missed or made before you ever hit the ball. If you go through your routine and follow the steps just like you've practiced, you won't have any trouble pulling the trigger. And a good percentage of putts will fall.

YOUR TEMPO SETS THE TONE.

Tempo is a popular topic for putting gurus. But you know what? Once you have a consistent routine and rhythm drilled deep into your subconscious mind, tempo probably won't be an issue at all. It will just flow naturally, with no conscious effort whatsoever.

Tempo is a great term to use in putting because you can probably relate it to the rest of your game. Some players, like Ernie Els and Fred Couples, have a slow, easy-going tempo in all their shots. Others, like Nick Price, do everything quickly, but not too quickly. The point is, your putting tempo should match the rest of your game.

You've all had days on the course when the tempo just seemed totally off — when your timing was so far gone you never knew where the ball was going to go. Tempo is just as important on the putting green. If you get too quick, you're going to miss. If you get too slow and deliberate, same thing. It's as simple as that. But we don't usually attribute missed putts to poor tempo. Usually we say we "looked up" or "pushed it" when in fact, poor tempo might have been the root of the problem.

If you want to get technical about it, smooth tempo means that the putter is traveling the same speed on the backswing as it is on the follow-through. If you take it back too quickly you're likely to decelerate coming through. If you take it back too slowly you're likely to get quick and jerky going through.

The way Ben Crenshaw's putter moves so fluidly back and through is truly phenomenal. The club just seems to pour through the ball, sending it rolling on the prettiest path you've ever seen. And the tempo never varies. No matter how long or short the putt is, the clubhead always takes its own, sweet time. There's never a hit or a hurried stroke. There's nothing mechanical about it. It's pure poetry.

Some people would have you believe that your backswing has to be the exact same length as your follow-through. Forget about it. If your tempo is well tuned the length of the swing in either direction will be fine. You'll never have to think about it.

Smooth, rhythmic tempo will naturally eliminate any problems you might have with deceleration — or "quitting"— at impact. Good tempo allows you to hit "through the ball" every time without ever thinking about it. As George Low once said, "rhythm is as important to putting as it is to Nureyev's dancing. "

> "My overriding objective in putting is to develop a feeling of fluidity, yet firmness, at impact... The key to this sensation lies far less in the mechanics of the stroke than in its tempo."
> **-Jack Nicklaus**

The right tempo will also dramatically improve your distance control. That's what instructors mean when they talk about letting the length of the stroke dictate the distance. Rather than using a short stroke and then increasing the tempo of the hit for the lag putts, it's best to maintain the same, even tempo and just lengthen the stroke. But be careful. If you start thinking about how long the stroke is — how far back you're taking it — you'll get yourself completely discombobulated. Just forget about it and focus on your tempo. The length of the stroke will take care of itself.

I've seen people practicing with a metronome, trying to sync-up their stroke… tick tock tick tock. Forget about it. Don't practice tempo out of context. If you think your tempo needs work, focus on the rhythm of your entire putting routine from beginning to end. Practice doing all those little steps in the same time frame every time and chances are, your tempo will take care of itself.

GET COMFORTABLE WITH YOUR READ OF THE GREEN.

Severe undulations and super fast, multi-tiered greens make a lot of pretty good players uncomfortable. In fact, many of the modern variations in putting technique can be traced to the speed of the greens that tour players encounter week in and week out.

Modern greens demand a much more subtle touch than the greens Hogan and Snead were accustomed to. These days, it's not uncommon to find greens that run 10 or 11 on the stimpmeter, even at public courses. (Believe me, that's fast!) In an effort to handle the speed, many pros have started tinkering with different techniques. They want a lighter touch, better distance control and absolutely no wrist action.

In Central Oregon, you could play several local courses without ever looking at a straight putt. Everything, it seems, moves drastically one direction or another, over a shoulder or up a tier. And I'm convinced that those crazy, roller-coaster greens contributed to my case of the yips. I was just too apprehensive about the line to hit the putts confidently, and one thing led to another. If you're in the same boat, find a nice flat practice green and start there. Once you've regained your confidence on the straight ones you can start working on the downhill, left-to-right breakers.

One of the most common tips you'll see about playing breaking putts is to pick an intermediate target at the apex of the curve. That way you can forget about the break and just play the putt as if it's straight. That's all fine and dandy, but what about speed? You can hit your preliminary target dead on and still miss by a mile if you hit it too hard, or worse yet, too soft. A lot more putts are missed short than missed wide right. Speed always dictates the break, not the other way around.

Green reading is an elusive art. It's takes a good eye combined with a keen intuitive sense and trust that comes with experience. You can analyze a putt every which way, but it always comes down to how well you trust your instincts. Or conversely, how much doubt you have. If you doubt how much a putt is going to break you're not going to be comfortable over the ball. Forget about it. On the putting green the slightest hint of doubt will doom your best effort. Once you pick a preliminary target you have to trust it enough to forget about the hole and stroke it at the target. Beyond that, the results depend entirely on speed and a good bit of luck.

Trust is also important when your intuition is overridden by experience. Play a course often enough and you'll file away some local knowledge that tells you the downhill putt on number seven doesn't really break toward the water like you'd expect. You have to trust your experience, pick a spot, and just let it roll. Despite the visual input that's telling you to hit it three inches left, you have to just hit it straight.

I wish we could teach you how to read greens in three simple steps, but we can't. You can't learn it overnight, you'll never learn it just from reading books or magazines, and you'll never do it right every time. Even the pros who have the help of veteran caddies misread putts occasionally.

> "A lot of golfers get themselves in a real tangle on breaking putts. First, they have an alignment problem at address and then they tend to want to guide the ball. It's a recipe for a lot of badly struck, badly missed putts."
>
> **-Ernie Els**

So why not accept the fact that's it's tricky and take a putting lesson? Get with a pro who can walk around a green with you and show you, first hand, how speed dictates break. No amount of reading can match the value of one good, hands-on demonstration. It's the only way you'll grasp the importance of speed over direction

No matter how much you practice reading greens you will encounter putts from time to time that you simply cannot figure out. I've been playing a course regularly for seven years and there's one green that still mystifies me every time. The ball just doesn't seem to follow any laws of nature or any logic at all. In cases like that, you have to go with your best guess. But here's the trick: you also have to fake it really well. You have to putt as if you're absolutely sure you have the break nailed. Pick a preliminary target, go through your normal, confident routine, and make a good assertive stroke. You'll be surprised how many of those wild guesses work out as long as you don't second guess yourself once you're over the putt.

THE FORGET-ABOUT-IT GUIDE TO PUTTING

GET COMFORTABLE WITH THE VOICES IN YOUR HEAD.

Volumes have been written on the state of mind you need to perform well in this game. "Stay in the present." "Be attentive yet unconscious." "Stay positive." "See it, feel it, trust it." "Strategize, visualize, actualize." "Maintain a state of benign imperturbability." It all applies to putting.

Although the language varies dramatically, one common theme comes through loud and clear: you simply can't putt and think at the same time. Forget about it. If you're still in an analytical, left-brained frame of mind when you get over the ball you're going to be in big trouble.

Analysis is fine as long as it takes place during your pre-shot routine. It's crucial, in fact. But when it comes to making the stroke, you have to turn it off and switch sides. It's the Player that controls your tempo, your feel and your ability to visualize the line. Somehow you have to shift gears from thinking to trusting, and just let the stroke happen naturally.

Probably the most common thought that haunts the average player is simply, "don't miss." For some reason, the imaginary repercussions of missing that little three footer just beat the positive thoughts into submission. And it's pretty hard to get comfortable when there are a thousand little voices in your head all screaming "DON'T MISS, DON'T MISS, DON'T MISS."

When you're standing over a double-breaking 50-footer it's easy to focus simply on making a good stroke. The voices are pretty quiet because your expectations are fairly low. But when you have a downhill, four-footer coming back, it's a different story altogether. The shorter the putt, the louder the voices get.

There are a couple ways to relax and silence the voices in your head — besides taking valium. The easiest way is to just have fun. If you're putting for birdie or eagle or even par it'll be easy. Just smile to yourself and think about how much fun it is just to have those opportunities. Regardless of the outcome. If you're putting for triple bogey it might be a little more difficult, but still doable. Just smile and think about how much fun it is to save yourself with your putter. Yeah, you can hack it around in the trees and still score if your putter's working well.

"The task of your mind is to give your body the guidance of a bright, vivid visual image, and then let it rip. Create the image and go."
- Dave Pelz

Ernie Els says he's never met an amateur who enjoys practicing putting. Not one. That's probably because most people have forgotten how to have fun on the putting green. They get so darn serious about improving their putting stroke they forget that it's still a game.

Let's face it, if you spend every moment of practice in an analysis mode, dissecting every little detail of your setup and stroke, it's not going to be a whole lot of fun. And what's more, you'll be developing the bad habit of thinking constantly about the mechanics of your stroke. When you get out on the course it's almost impossible to turn it off.

Forget about spending a lot of time grinding away on the putting green. Instead, find a friend who you can give you a good game.

Be creative. The best practice is the practice that most closely replicates a real round of golf, so put some pressure on yourself. Play for quarter skins or something like that. There's nothing better than a little friendly competition to simulate real course conditions.

Another fun way to sharpen your putting skill is to take your kids to one of those natural-turf putting courses. Many of the new upscale public courses and resorts have them. Or better yet, work on your entire short game by playing a little chip & putt course. That'll really test your skill on the greens. Quit working at it, and start playing again.

The other way to calm your mind and free yourself of those pesky voices is to make sure you're comfortable with all the variables we've just discussed. If you're comfortable with the club you're using, the putting method and the line, the mental approach will pretty much take care of itself. The negative thoughts will be replaced by a calm sense of security that comes from one thing: confidence in your fundamentals.

FORGET ABOUT THE ROBO-PUTTERS AND PENDULUMS.

If you've ever read anything on putting you've probably been exposed to conflicting information that represents one of the longest running debates in golf. Should you take the putter straight back and through, or should you let it go a little inside on the way back and then "release" the clubhead on the follow-through? Is the path of the putter supposed to be straight, or is it an arc?

There are two schools of thought on this, and there have been great putters from both schools. Ben Crenshaw's gorgeous putting stroke is a stunning example of the natural arc. Jack Nicklaus, on the other hand, takes the putter head straight back pushes it straight through in a piston-like motion.

Obviously, either method can work, and it depends entirely on your personal preference. If you've always putted straight back and straight through, we wouldn't advise changing. However, if you're just taking up the game or if you've been stricken with the yips, it's best to go with the simplest, most natural swing, which is an arc.

My old, Nicklaus-style putting method worked pretty well as long as I kept the backswing really short. I made a lot of five-footers that way. (I had to because my lag putts never seemed to snuggle up very close to the hole.) Come to find out, that's a pretty common problem for people who putt that way. Straight back and through works great on short putts, but it's hard to make a long stroke that stays perfectly square all the way. The clubhead wants to move to the inside naturally, which means you have to consciously try to keep the putter on line. And conscious effort of any kind can be deadly.

That's another thing that contributed to my yips. When I lengthened my backswing to match the follow-through, which every article endorses, I got really fixated on taking the putter straight back. Short and straight was fine, but long and straight just didn't work. I had to consciously think about keeping the putter on line. To do that, I started pushing the clubhead back rather than swinging it. That's when the train jumped the tracks.

I started making all sorts of adjustments — or more accurately, spastic manipulations — to hit the ball squarely. The harder I tried to putt straight back and straight through, the more mechanical it got. My lag putting didn't improve, and I started missing a lot of short putts. Then my confidence went out the window.

Proponents of the straight, square to square method often use the analogy of a perfect pendulum. Forget about it. The whole concept of the pendulum swing is misleading, at best, and we believe it should be stricken from the golfing vocabulary.

A pendulum hangs vertically. In croquet, you use a true pendulum motion for those between-the-leg shots. But the minute you stand to one side to "send" your opponent's ball from here to kingdom come, the pendulum thing goes out the window. Same with putting. There's not a putter in the world that hangs down perfectly straight. Even the long, chin-type putters have a little angle to them.

In 1973 the editors of Golf Digest summed it up quite well in a book called "All About Putting… "It might appear that the ideal putting backswing would carry the clubhead back from the ball in a absolutely straight line. This would be true, however, only if the stroke were started with the hands directly over the ball, with the shaft of the putter perfectly perpendicular to the ground. Then a true pendulum stroke could be achieved, but it would be an awkward and unnatural stroke."

The pendulum concept causes confusion and forces people into all sorts of unnatural positions. People take it way too literally. In a hopeless effort to get the shaft of the club pointing straight up and down — like an actual pendulum — they either stand up way too straight, or they hunch over too much. They never get comfortable.

Another problem with this analogy is that pendulums are inherently rigid and mechanical. We have a hard time with these so-called scientific studies that use robots to test the ideal putting stroke. Are there any robots in your foursome? I don't think so. You can't get comfortable putting like a robot.

> "If my putter shaft were perfectly upright at address, it could pre-cisely reproduce the action of a pendulum. The shaft, however, extends at an angle toward me, which means that the clubhead does not fol-low a straight-back, straight-through line. Its natural path of move-ment is inside the line on the backswing and inside it again on the followthrough."
>
> **-Bob Charles**

Another visual analogy that's been around for a long time is the swinging of a large gate. If the gate only opens a crack, the curve is pretty slight, but it's still there. If the gate opens wide, like on a long, lag putt, there's a more pronounced curve. But the swinging of a gate is perfectly horizontal. The swinging of a pendulum is per-fectly vertical. Neither accurately reflects the swinging of a putter.

So forget about it. Just let the putter swing naturally and for-get about the swing plane altogether. As long as your arms are ten-sion-free, and you swing naturally without any manipulation of the clubhead with your hands, the swing path will take care of itself. It naturally moves a bit inside the line, and the clubface will appear slightly open when you reach the end of the backswing.

FORGET ABOUT THE TOUR STATS AND GET SOME GOALS OF YOUR OWN.

Most people assume that watching the best players in the world sinking clutch putts will help their own putting. Don't bet on it. Sure, seeing Brad Faxon pouring them in or Tiger Woods charging them into the back of the cup can leave a nice impression of the ultimate possibilities. But watching the Sunday telecasts of major tournaments might actually mess up your head more than it will smooth out your stroke.

At the 2003 Player's Championship, Davis Love shot a blistering 64 in the final round to win by 6 strokes. Afterward, he said it was the best round he's ever played in competition, and attributed his success to his putting. "It seemed like every time I looked up the ball was going in the middle of the hole." Love made everything that day. Literally. He had 13 putts from inside 8 feet and made every one. He made 5 birdies in a row, plus a 15-footer for eagle. He carded only 27 putts.

Ben Crane won his first PGA tour event — The BellSouth Classic — with 23 putts on Saturday and 24 putts on Sunday, including a 20-footer for eagle on the 18th hole. That's 47 putts in 36 holes!

Retief Goosen won the 2004 U.S. Open at Shinnecock Hills by carding only 24 putts on Sunday. That type of performance has a way of skewing our expectations when it comes to putting. You can easily lose site of reality because you never see the guys who are putting poorly. (They aren't in contention and the networks only cover the contenders.) So all weekend you watch the leaders who are putting the lights out and you start thinking, "why don't I make more of those 8-footers? What am I doing wrong? Maybe I should try that claw grip." You start wondering, and wondering leads directly to experimenting, which leads to discomfort, which leads to tension, which leads to misses.

Forget about it. What you have to realize is that even the tour pros — the best players in the world —miss half of those 8-footers. Fifty percent! And 10-footers… Only one in three. So don't get too hung up on the tour stats. Don't compare yourself to what those guys are doing on TV, it's just not realistic.

Part of the problem with golf is how we evaluate performance. In other sports there is a clear cut standard of perfection. In tennis you can play a set without losing a game, or even a point. In ice skating you can get straight 6.0's from every judge. In bowling all you have to do is roll 12 straight strikes. In baseball there's the no-hitter. But in golf, mastery is much more elusive.

Some people contend that 54 on a par-72 course would be a "perfect" score. Others believe that 18 birdies wouldn't do it, that you'd have to throw in four eagles just for good measure. Forget about it. The number is not the point. The point is to better yourself, because in this game the bar is always moving.

When it comes to putting, what you should do is keep track of all your putts in every round and set some tangible, achievable goals for yourself. Establish a personal par for putting, and try to beat that. That's how you measure your own performance. If you meet that goal you'll probably find yourself playing consistently at or below your handicap.

Interestingly, higher handicap players — in the 12 to 20 range — can realistically expect to take fewer putts than a low handicapper. That's because the lower handicap player hits more greens in regulation and is left with a lot of lag putts. The higher handicap player, who isn't as sharp with the irons, misses most of the greens in regulation and ends up chipping to the hole. In this case, if you're still taking 36 putts a round you probably won't be very happy with your scores. 30 might be a better target.

> "A lot of instructional talk today comes out of the rare air in which a couple of hundred unusually gifted and highly trained touring pros operate, and really contributes little or nothing useful to the game of the weekend golfer."
>
> **–Sam Snead**

Most people would just say they want to quit three-putting, and that's a good place to start. But the question is, what's causing those three-putts? What are you going to work on to reach the goal? Is it poor lag putting, or do you have a major synaptic accident every time you're faced with a three-and-a-half-footer coming back?

The fact is, you have to be a little lucky to sink a lot of putts. Some days the luck will be on your side, and other days it'll seem like there's a force-field protecting the cup. What you have to do is accept the fickle nature of it and move on. If you miss, just write it off as bad luck. Look at it this way. With every putt you miss the odds increase that you'll make the next one. Just keep telling yourself that you're due to sink one, and eventually you will.

Remember, the goal is to have fun out there. If you're always beating yourself up for not putting as well as Tiger Woods, you're going to be miserable.

After years of frustration and downright humiliation on the greens, I'm having fun with it again. I don't "putt" the ball at all, that's way too hard. I just line it up and let it happen. And some of them are actually going in. I'm getting more and more positive feedback every day. The hole looks much bigger to me now and I know that as long as I keep practicing my fundamentals, my stroke will continue to improve. But I'm not thinking about that.

THE FORGET-ABOUT-IT EPILOGUE

Ever since I started working on this book I've been waiting for that one magical round that would be the inspiration for the final chapter. Every time I drive to the golf course I envision a fairy tale ending where all of Andy's coaching and all my practice and all the advice of this book come together into one flawless round of pars, birdies, eagles and aces.

Well forget about it. This isn't fiction, and as much as I like happy endings I'm not going to conjure up something just for the sake of vanity. My journey's just begun. Andy has shown me how to tap into my natural talent — my wealth of potential — but I've only scratched the surface. And I have to keep reminding myself to just forget about that last shot. Forget about all those swing keys I used to employ. Forget about the takeaway and the top position and the leg action and the hip rotation.

Too much thinking is still my single biggest problem. Always will be. But I'm a different player now. When I'm standing over a putt the hole looks ten times bigger than it used to. When I have a bad hole, it's not nearly as bad as it used to be. And I'm much better at bouncing back after a minor mental lapse. I know that if I just quit trying so darn hard, it will happen.

I'm probably more passionate about the game than ever, but I don't play as much. I don't practice as much either, and when I do it's much more productive than ever before. No more experimentation. No more searching for the answer every time out. Now I know what I need to work on, and I do it. It's not rocket science, just fun-DUH-mentals every time out.

Bad rounds don't torment me like they did a couple years ago. I used to dwell on those days, replaying every bad shot in my head. Then I'd go to the driving range to correct whatever it was that was plaguing me. Now I'm able to just forget about it. Unfortunately my scores haven't consistently reflected my new-found confidence, but I know they will. And maybe that's the difference. I know they will.

Most of the change is in my head, but it manifests itself in a tighter swing and some pretty decent play on the golf course. And there was one round that came pretty close to the fantasy ending that I envisioned.

It was one of those autumn evenings in Central Oregon when every breath just seems like a divine gift of unimaginable proportions.

Rain showers had awakened the pungent smell of sage and juniper. Ominous, black clouds were giving way to a blinding sun that was setting behind the Cascade Mountains. I was all alone on the course, and as I teed it up on the first hole a brilliant rainbow appeared directly over the fairway. By the time I walked to my ball — which had sailed obediently down the middle — a rare, double rainbow had formed. Two perfect arches framed the green as if I had scripted the scene for a made-for-TV movie. What an omen! If I had had my camera with me I could have sold the photo a million times over.

As I prepared for my next shot I was thinking, "this has got to be THE round." The scene was just too perfect. With a 9-iron in my hand, I was looking at an easy birdie, but the approach leaked out to the right, a good 40 feet from the pin. A good lag putt and it was a kick-in par. Not exactly epic, but still a fine start.

The second tee is elevated and faces back to the west, toward the mountains and straight into the setting sun. My drive felt good, but I couldn't see it at all. I grabbed my bag and headed straight down the fairway — there was never a doubt where I'd find it. I just couldn't miss. Another 9-iron in, and this time I hit it as pure as the Oregon air. Unfortunately it should have been a wedge and I short-sided myself, leaving a nasty, downhill pitch back to the pin. I hit a good, high shot and was left with 10 feet for par. No problem. I went through my new, six-step routine and stroked the ball straight as an arrow into the middle of the cup.

After that miracle par I was definitely feeling the magic. The twin rainbows were getting even more intense as I played the par-5 third. When I hit a lob wedge to about eight feet I thought, "this is it, the pot of gold." But the birdie eluded me thanks to a bad read and it was on to number four. Even par so far.

Standing on the tee of the 150-yard par-3 I was thinking hole-in-one. For the first time in my life I was thinking realistically about hitting the ball in the hole from the tee. Just an 8-iron with a little draw to that back pin and it's in. Nothing to it. When I swung it felt perfect, and as it sailed up through the prism-colored sky I thought it had a chance. It landed three feet from the cup, but much to my dismay bounced high and kicked off the back of the green. Short sided again. Another lucky, scrambling par.

On the next tee I could feel the moment slipping away. The rainbow had drifted off to the north and my drive headed south, into the heavy rough. But I managed to find the green with my approach, and another good lag putt kept the streak alive.

Somewhere between the fifth green and the sixth tee, the unthinkable happened. Something even worse than playing the wrong ball or leaving a wedge three holes back. Yes, it was my cell phone, piercing the peaceful surroundings from the deepest pocket of my golf bag. It sounded worse than the most obnoxious pre-dawn alarm clock. How could I forget to turn it off? Naturally, it was my wife, and it was not good news. As she talked I could feel the wind seeping out of my proverbial sails. I commiserated with her and chatted nicely for a couple minutes. Then I hung up and tried to regroup. But the damage was done. My train of thought was totally derailed.

The next hole's an easy little par-4 with a sharp dogleg to the right. I just didn't recall how sharp until I hit driver straight through the fairway into a gnarly old juniper tree. Two club lengths for an unplayable lie weren't quite enough, and before I knew it I carded a double-bogey. So much for the fairy tale ending. One lousy phone call and the whole story line was shot.

Walking to the next tee I told myself to just forget about it. It was just one hole, one minor mental lapse. I could still bounce back — make a couple birdies coming in and still have what I was hoping for. But that's not how it happened. I missed a legitimate birdie opportunity on the next hole, then bogeyed the par-3 eighth, so I was three over par going into the ninth hole.

The light was fading fast as I walked down to the ninth tee. The sun was gone, along with the rainbow that had followed me around those first several holes. But I was determined to finish strong. A simple par would keep my score in the thirties, which for me is always a good 9-hole goal.

My tee ball started out a little right of the intended line and disappeared into the twilight. I found it in the thick rough and then slashed it back out into the fairway, leaving about 125 yards into a tiny little green. At that point I was still brimming with confidence. Even after the bogey on the last hole I was still holding out hope that something spectacular was going to happen. Eagle was entirely possible.

The last full shot of the day sailed straight at the flagstick, and for just a second I thought it might be in. (I couldn't see that it landed 20 feet short.) Two easy putts later and that was it. An anticlimactic par on an easy par-5.

No matter. In the scheme of things, my score seems totally irrelevant. It was the promise of the whole experience that sticks with me to this day. There was an aura of success that couldn't be dampened, despite a cell phone call and a tee shot into the trees. I got an inspiring glimpse of my true potential and an awesome display of mother nature, all in the span of a few holes. And if you forget about all the other nonsense, isn't that what golf's all about?

REFERENCED MATERIALS

All About Putting by the editors of Golf Digest

And If You Play Golf, You're My Friend by Harvey Penick & Bud Shrake

Be the Ball Charlie Jones & Kim Doren

Down The Fairway by Robert T. "Bobby" Jones Jr. & O.B. Keller

For All Who Love The Game by Harvey Penick & Bud Shrake

Going Low by Patrick Cohen

Golf For Enlightenment by Deepak Chopra

Golf Is Not A Game Of Perfect by Bob Rotella

Golf My Way by Jack Nicklaus

Golfers On Golf by Downs MacRury

Harvey Penick's Little Red Book by Harvey Penick & Bud Shrake

How To Become A Complete Golfer by Jim Flick & Bob Toski

Mind Over Golf by Richard Coop & Bill Fields

Natural Golf by Sam Snead

On Golf by Jim Flick

On Learning Golf by Percy Boomer

Putt Like The Pros by Dave Pelz

Rethinking Golf by Chuck Hogan

See It And Sink It by Craig L. Farnsworth

Swing The Clubhead by Ernest Jones

The Complete Short Game by Ernie Els

The Golfer's Book of Daily Inspiration by Kevin Nelson

The Golfer's Book Of Wisdom by Criswell Freeman

The Heart Of A Golfer by Wally Armstrong

The Inner Game Of Golf by Timothy Gallway

The Mental Art Of Putting by Patrick Cohen & Robert K. Winters

The New Golf Mind by Gary Wiren & Richard Coop

SHARE THE FORGET-ABOUT-IT GUIDE
WITH ALL YOUR GOLFING BUDDIES.

Get one for every person in your foursome. Order on line at www.forgetaboutitgolf.com. If you're interested in bulk orders or if you'd like to have a Forget-About-It Golf clinic at your club, call or e-mail john@forgetaboutitgolf.com.

ABOUT THE AUTHORS

John Furgurson has the mind of a writer and the spirit of an entrepreneur. He's written just about anything he could charge a fair rate for, including ad copy, corporate video scripts, radio commercials, speeches, magazine articles and even an occasional infomercial. Currently he's a partner at V, a venture creative firm in Bend, Oregon. With the right sunglasses on, he looks a lot like David Duval.

Andy Heinly has a natural talent for the game, and a remarkable gift for teaching. If he's not giving golf lessons or opening a new course, he's probably coaching a little league basketball, baseball or football team. Currently he's Head Golf Professional at Eagle Crest Resort in Redmond, Oregon. His greatest claim to fame is the Heinly Maneuver, used only in the most extreme cases of golfer distress.